Living a Prosperous Life

WALKING IN THE LIGHT OF GRACE

Living a Prosperous Life

WALKING IN THE LIGHT OF GRACE

LARRY BACHMAN

CITI OF BOOKS

CITIOFBOOKS, INC.
3736 Eubank NE Suite A1
Albuquerque, NM 87111-3579
www.citiofbooks.com
Hotline: 1 (877) 389-2759
Fax: 1 (505) 930-7244

Ordering Information:
Quantity sales. Special discounts are available on quantity purchases by corporations, associations, and others. For details, contact the publisher at the address above.

Printed in the United States of America.

ISBN-13:   Softcover   979-8-89391-202-9
                eBook   979-8-89391-203-6

Library of Congress Control Number: 2024914392

TABLE OF CONTENTS

FOREWORD

I have known Larry Bachman now for about ten years. His creativity and imagination in Christian writing brings clarity and a close experience with the plot. Larry Bachman has a special gift for making the truths within the Bible come alive and simple to understand. Packaged within riveting true stories, Larry brings the kingdom life right into what we experience today. There is no room for the abstract with Larry. The kingdom of God, as he explains, is distant, yet it is also near. *Living a Prosperous Life … Walking in the Light of Grace* is a life transforming book. Rather than living life unfilled and unsatisfied, full of stress and awaiting life in heaven, this book says we can live the life hope for now. The key to this life, as stated by Larry, is Jesus. Jesus said, "In this manner, therefore, pray:

Our Father in heaven,

Hallowed be Your name.

Your kingdom come.

Your will be done

On earth as it is in heaven." (Matthew 6:9–10, NKJV)

Jesus wants us to experience the kingdom life here on earth. Larry points out that He wants to give us a purpose, a healthy body, mind, and spirit, a legacy and much more. "When you trust in Christ and begin to more and more take on God's intended character, you become a light to a dark world. You will begin to reflect the life of Christ and submit to the will of God the Father. When you put God first you spend time in prayer, serve others and think of yourself less. Soon you will say; not my will, but your will Lord, not my glory, but for your glory Lord. The things you are willing do in His name is for the advancement of God's kingdom on earth."

This is a must read and a highly spiritual and empowering book. Enjoy.

—Pastor Sean A. Harris is an ordained minister of the Seventh-day Adventist Church. He currently serves as Senior Pastor for the Mansfield SDA Church and English Men's Ministry Director for the Texas Conference of Seventh-day Adventists. He holds a master's in divinity from Andrews University, as well as a BS and MS in Electrical Engineering from Texas A&M University and Prairie View A&M University, respectively.

PREFACE

From the Homestead ...

A very dear friend of mine, "Pastor Sean Harris of the Mansfield, Texas SDA," verbally grabbed my ear one day as he said, "Larry, I need your help."

Cautiously I asked, "What about, do you need my help?"

Replying he stated, "I need you to help me write a book."

"Oh really," as I curiously ventured forward. "A book ... and you, who have not even a moment to sit down and eat, will have how much time for contribution?"

And so it goes ... this is the Lord's work. Pastor Sean's contributions, his suggestions, advisements, prayer—they are in here. The Lord gave Pastor Sean a mission, and Pastor Sean gave me direction to what people needed to find in the pages of our book. Pastor Sean and I are brothers-in-arms for Christ within the fabric of His ministry and mission. Praise the Lord!

Life's a journey, and everyone has a story to tell. Switchbacks and button hooks has my adventure been, but here I am still standing to tell and pass forward my experiences. I pray this book will benefit, give hope and encouragement, and bring to those who deem themselves fearfully lost a message from the Lord and Savior. Matthew 11:28–30 says, "Come unto me, all ye that labour and are heavy laden, and I will give you rest. Take my yoke upon you, and learn of me; for I am meek and lowly in heart: and ye shall find rest unto your souls. For my yoke is easy, and my burden is light."

My dear, late mother once had words for me. She looked me straight in the eye and uttered, "Larry, I will pray for you."

This was after a very troublesome time I had with the law. Oh yes, little old me. Confession tends to help, so I bare my soul, toss to the side any preconceptions you might have in thinking I am perfect from a life of never having been in the trenches fighting worldly battles. That particular war, of course, was due to my own unnecessary foolishness. But that is an entirely different time and circumstance and another book perhaps.

Samuel Clemmons, pen name "Mark Twain," once said, "There are two very important dates that should be noted in everyone's life. First; when you are born and secondly when you discover the reason why." Mr. Clemmons, while in Seattle, Washington, was approached by a young man who asked, "Sir, how do you come up with these interesting stories to tell? I too want to be a writer."

"Son, how old are you?" asked Clemmons.

"Well sir, I just turned nineteen," was the young man's reply.

"I see," said Mr. Clemmons, "My advice, son, is for you to take a little more time out of life, stop the book learning for a while, and add to that some real living, then you can write about those experiences."

The young man took Samuel Clemmons' advice and headed North to Alaska and later wrote the book *White Fang*. The lad's name was Jack London.

We as a family are now one less as our youngest went off to college and has made us "empty nester homesteaders." Being one short does not allow us any slack in daily duties. We are still trying to figure out what goes and what stays in our garden planting design. Our ultimate goal is to sell what we grow. It has been a challenge.

Watermelons were planted too close to squash, and our busy honeybees did a wonderful job of pollinating. They crossed our squash with the melons and cantaloupes. Hopefully their honey will provide good compensation for the melon/squash debacle. We still enjoyed making slushies from the melons and the taste was curiously refreshing. You never stop learning.

We have learned much from our goose family this year. They are by design a very interesting group of web-footed, feathered friends … and better at intruder alert than most pet dogs! On occasion there has been a sick goose. It is amazing that the others will hover about and patiently wait to see what is the matter with their sister. We came home one day to find that one of the geese had gotten stuck in the gate. As soon as we got out of the car we were alerted by the resounding honking of the entire family. *Come see! Come see!* They seemed to call out. We did, and discovered the problem. They waited for their compatriot to be loosed from the entanglement and recovered before they moved towards the pond. As they moved out, they waited for the hurt one to catch up as it seemed to be in pain and would sit down often. In caring they showed courtesy. When the hurt goose was ready and moved forward, so did they all, in one family group.

We also must be aware of our surroundings and listen to the cries of those around us, be they silent or outspoken. We, too, must come to the aid of our brothers and sisters who need to be loosed from distress.

There are many people I need to thank at this point. First, I want to thank Pastor Sean for placing trust in me to complete this task. I want to thank my wife, Claudia, for affording me the time that is necessary to take on such an endeavor. Also to those who have given me strength and encouragement over the years, my daughters Sheinny and Larayne, my son Benjamin, and to all my friends both near and far … thank you, thank you. And tantamount to everyone and everything else I thank my producer, my publicist, and my inspiration the Lord and Savior Jesus Christ, for without Him nothing ever gets completed to provide fruition.

The majority of the stories which are imbedded within this book are true. Names have been changed and definitive places have been altered to retain privacy. They are true experiences none-the-less. A blessing is what I hope you find within as it was a blessing for me to write.

CHAPTER 1

Oh Heaven, Where Art Thou?

On any given day on planet earth, as the sun rises, the world wakes up and reacts to decisions made by countless people. At internet speed, information travels around the globe, affecting change beyond our own spheres of reality. This process is done in order to influence what we purchase, what we say, what we do, where we go, who we vote for—and in the end, how we think—affecting perception of the quality and nature of our own lives.

As we react to these pushed influences, our responses give cause to act, and thus our actions bring about our choices. These choices make and define our character. What we choose to do engenders consequences and accountability. That which is chosen shows who and what we represent.

Since the dawn of time man has searched the vast heavens for answers. Seated beneath the greatest illuminated canopy imaginable, early man found vast creatures in the starry sky that played out dramas folded within the night. They were not navigators to point the way home, but were individual souls left to dream alone and ponder. With eyes steadfast on the circling night sky, at first content, they remained stardust, earthbound misfits that would one day wish to take flight.

Galileo discovered four of Jupiter's moons four hundred years ago. Sir Isaac Newton, a great mathematician, physicist, and astronomer stated, "I can calculate the movement of the heavenly bodies but not the insanity of people." We cannot forget Leonardo Di Vinci, the man of renaissance, who designed flying machines, calculated, and brought forth the evidence—man could fly. Leonardo said, "When once you have tasted flight, you will forever walk the earth with your eyes turned skyward for there you have been and there you will always long to return." There were the Wright brothers at Kitty Hawk, North Carolina, who in 1909 took their "Wright Flyer" on its successful trial run.

On September 5, 1977, Voyager 1 was launched by NASA to study our immediate solar system and beyond. It has been on mission now for over forty years and on August 25, 2012, it was the first spacecraft to cross the heliopause (the boundary of the heliosphere) and enter interstellar space. Man has, in an attempt to better understand his relationship with the cosmos, built incredible telescopes, surrounded our planet with satellites and space stations, sent men to the moon, and sent spacecraft to catalogue, photograph, gather soil samples, and send data back to our earth-bound laboratories.

Several thousand years ago three wise men called *Magi* diligently gazed at the stars, watching for a sign, and followed a star to a small town called Bethlehem, fulfilling a prophetic message.

What if today—right here and right now on planet earth—you already hold the keys to take flight? You who are stardust and earth bound actually have the means to achieve just that: freedom and heaven on earth.

What if today—right here and right now on planet earth—you already hold the keys to take flight? You who are stardust and earth bound actually have the means to achieve just that: freedom and heaven on earth. This means is not just for you personally, but will affect everyone around you ... your spouse, children, parents, grandparents, friends, and neighbors. You will become the foundation of your heavenly ark, if you will.

This is good news ... right? Believe it—you hold the keys in your hand to unlock the door and all you then have to do is walk through.

Never again will you feel like a king without castle or a queen without a throne, because now you will be moving on. You can say, "No more will I listen to what once was considered undisputed truth. I am part of a new horizon; I will shine like a star. My life will be made anew. I will not look behind me now; my troubles will be few."

You can say goodbye to all those friends who have become strangers, who by their suggestions of paradise and dreams have faded away along with everything else, with their promises that have never come true. You will be able to laugh at those who have said, "You're bonkers; the devil is your savior."

Who do they think they are fooling? You will wonder. All this time they have been saying, "We are having fun!" But you kept on going nowhere until you realized it has been a waste of precious time. You've chased almighty dollars and helped them achieve the perfect crime. The dangling carrot made you follow—you drank the wretched wine, poisoning the body, poisoning the mind. They fed you their lies, making you believe it tasted good. It came by news, internet, and phone ... why did you do this? Because the medium told you that you should.

Here are a few questions for you, and to yourself you must be true. Can you keep going down the same road time and time and time again and expect to find a different scenario? That's three times you have been down the same path. Einstein suggested that after three trials and experiments, why should you expect something different a fourth time? Huh?

I heard someone say, "There must be something better ... there must be something more." Well, if there is, it exists within you. Get up and do something about it. Stop running away from your destiny. Face it, embrace it, and remember, wherever you go—THERE—YOU—ARE. YOU are the only one who can make a difference, who can do something about it. It's your future and YOU hold the key. Now open the door!

What key is that and how do I do it? I'm glad you asked!

1 Peter 2:9–10 says, "But ye are a chosen generation, a royal priesthood, an holy nation, a peculiar people; that ye should shew forth the praises of him who hath called you out of darkness into His marvellous light; Which in time past were not a people, but are now the people of God: which had not obtained mercy, but now have obtained mercy."

You = The Foundation, Mind, Body, and Spirit!

Foundation is described by Webster and Dictionary.com as follows:

1) The moral (**foundation**) of both religion and society.

2) The natural or prepared ground or base upon which a structure rests.

3) A usually stone or concrete structure that supports a building from underneath.

4) Something such as an idea, principle, or fact that provides support for something.

It will be on solid rock that you will stand because all other ground is shifting sand (Matt. 7:24–27). You will become the foundation upon which the structure of your life will be built. It's a brave new world out there which imprisons us, and you will come out from among it and be separate.

Okay, but how do I accomplish that? I've got a job, a wife, and kids. I've got responsibilities!

You are going down this path for all those reasons and if you are taking the time to read this book you have already become a responsible party. Nelson Mandela, for example, was arrested in South Africa and spent years in jail. But even though he was imprisoned physically, those responsible did not capture his soul; his spirit was caused to flourish, not just in that 6' x 9' cell, but the spark of his ideas flew outside those prison walls and caught fire. If they would have killed him, the governing body of that country would have to deal with a martyr.

Freedom starts as an idea as proven by the founding fathers of America. First it was whispered in secret meetings because it was so fragile. To actually have a government that is established by and for the good of the people seemed ludicrous. Having people govern themselves and elect only those who would serve the needs and wishes of those who put them in power sounded too much like Camelot—a place that only existed in a fairy tale.

Wouldn't those placed in those lofty positions be fearful of those who put them there if they did not fulfill their obligations? Yes, and they should be! Anything less than their best effort would be representative of tyranny. This crime of tyranny is the exact reason why people fled to America in the first place. Immigrants came to America in any way, shape, and form they could, all in an effort to escape religious persecution, starvation, war, and the suffering of it all. America beckoned to the masses: bring me your tired, oppressed, hungry, and poor of spirit.

Even so the pain remains today worldwide. Even within the borders of America with all its great freedoms and opportunities, there is still an overshadowing emptiness. All feel it in the pit of their stomachs aching to the far reaches of their hearts. We are drowning in the swill of emotional tyranny. We are imprisoned within a moral fog and we need to find the lighthouse that will guide us back and anchor us to solid rock.

Biblically there is an election to bring us out of our spiritual tyranny. You are elected to be saved from this malaise and it is the only election mentioned in the Word of God. Men have viewed the end times thinking that they were surely elected to Christendom and will spend eternity in heavenly bliss; the Bible does not mention such an election. We were elected by grace to work out our own salvation in fear of the Word of God.

Put on the armor of God and fight the good fight of faith. You are elected to choose and use the means that God has given to war against every unholy card that Satan deals us in the game of life for our souls. We must watch and pray as we are elected to search the Scriptures and plead, "Lord lead us not into temptation." Christians are elected to have unceasing faith and be obedient to every word that proceeds from out of the mouth of God, and be not just hearers only, but doers of the word.

In Matthew 6:7–13 Jesus taught us to pray to the Heavenly Father who watches over us from His heavenly kingdom: "Our Father which art in heaven, Hallowed be thy name. Thy kingdom come, Thy will be done [and where is this will to be done?] IN EARTH, as it is in heaven."

What surrounds us is religion—calling out to us everywhere and from almost every street corner—different faiths, different denominations, different pastors, small churches, medium churches, and of course the mega church where you can come and go as you please and perhaps no one will notice you. You will know, of course, and so does God. But most of the churchgoers won't take notice. You will be safe there, not seen, and if you so choose you don't ever have to go back. You could probably seat yourself in a different church all fifty-two weeks of any given year just on the premise of being a content church hopper or shopper on a mission of observation for the purpose of selection.

We are all broken—sick, tired, lonely, penniless, heartbroken—and the church is deemed the hospital. We the patients attend church for what reason? To be spiritually healed and uplifted, right? Many churches provide potluck at the end of service so if you have the need you won't go hungry.

So you ask—what is this religion thing all about? You won't find "religion" in this book's appendix. It ain't about religion. But it IS about relationship—the blessing of the Holy Spirit through Jesus Christ, who is the only head joined to our group. The difference between a Kingdom mindset and a worldly one is who is at the head, who is the King, who is in charge 24/7. Again, it is about building a relationship, not religion. This is where the foundation begins. Don't take these words for the undisputed truth; let's look at the Bible, for it is written.

Christ said in John 16:33, "These things I have spoken unto you, that in Me you might have peace. In the world you will have tribulation; but be of good cheer, I have overcome the world" (NKJV).

Exodus 19:5–8 says:

Now therefore, if ye will obey my voice indeed, and keep my covenant, then ye shall be a peculiar treasure unto me above all people: for all the earth is mine: And ye shall be unto me a kingdom of priests, and an holy nation. These are the words which thou shalt speak unto the children of Israel. And Moses came and called for the elders of the people, and laid before their faces all these words which the Lord commanded him. And all the people answered together, and said, All that the Lord hath spoken we will do. And Moses returned the words of the people unto the Lord.

And all the people answered together, and said—what? Curiously they left out the one person who could help them accomplish that goal. Because anything proposed by man alone is prone to fail. It should not have been answered, "WE WILL DO," but rather, "WITH GOD'S HELP WE WILL DO THESE THINGS."

So, my friend, as you start building your foundation put in place the cornerstone of prayer, asking God in Jesus' name to give you an ample supply of the Holy Spirit to see you through the day and each and every task you hope to accomplish.

You might also look at Exodus 19:5–8 and say, "Hey, it's talking about Moses and Israel there ... not me." We are the new Israel today because the covenant was passed to us when Israel, in the book of John, chapters 18 and 19, denied and crucified Christ. Yet, He did rise, did He not? And in rising, He passed that covenant on to all who believe. It is yours now to choose or not to choose—with God's help of course. If God be on your side, who or what can stand against you?

Jesus preached that what He delivered to the world was the kingdom government. We preach today the Good News of Heaven. However, the early church had it correct when they preached and taught that NOW is the time to establish the kingdom government on planet earth.

Don't get me wrong ... there is great joy in looking forward to being heaven-bound. But think about the fact that 75% or better of the earth's population is in a daily struggle for survival. It is necessary for the world to hear the good news of the Kingdom of Heaven (that being God's government). The rule of the Lord God has come to planet earth and

ALL can experience that reality. Again see John 16:33— "These things I have spoken unto you, that in me ye might have peace. In the world ye shall have tribulation: but be of good cheer; I have overcome the world."

Also consider Psalm 19:14, which says, "Let the words of my mouth, and the meditation of my heart, be acceptable in thy sight, O LORD, my strength, and my redeemer."

Remember, our Heavenly Father is holy and cannot compromise who He is. As representation of the heart of God on earth, we are the message. Our lives, stories, and history of us proclaiming who we are in the revelation of God speaks volumes on His behalf. We own that story—we are responsible. And don't we want to do our best to show Him as He really is? Of course, we do.

There is a heavenly plan for each and every one of us who can see the light. With this light we have the ability to bless, heal, and prosper so that we may be a blessing to all around us. It is up to you, once again, to choose to walk the path of righteousness. Once you know who you are in Christ you can then fulfill your God-given destiny. Take the first step and anchor your foundation to the Rock, Jesus Christ.

On the Fast Track …

There is a story about a young lady who we will name Karla. She believed she had it all together. Upon graduating college summa-cum-laude in record time, with a PhD and a law degree clasped tightly in hand, Karla left the ivory covered towers of higher learning behind.

Karla found all kinds of corporate offers coming her way but chose instead a career in law. Heartfelt, she believed in a higher calling— to represent the less fortunate people who had lost everything to misfortune. She truly felt this is where she was needed.

Hebrews 13:3 tells us, "Remember them that are in bonds, as bond with them; and them which suffer adversity, as being yourselves also in the body." (We are our brothers' and sisters' keeper, after all.)

However, the law firm she was licensed to placed Karla in representation of the high-paying, corporate clients. What she witnessed was appalling. At the merciless hands and rule of corporation bean counters, people out in the world were being taken advantage of. She witnessed that the big corporations had already folded into their earnings to account for litigation of shortcuts in safety, shoddy, short-sighted construction, and underhanded business practices.

Ignoring her still, small voice and her original intent, Karla pushed forward into the muck and mire of big money and the adoration of her peers. The months and years flew by, until one day the still young lady Karla looked into her personal handheld mirror. The lies and back stabbing that she knew was taking place, what Karla knew as being wrongfully represented, was now apparent in her face. As she took inventory, where once shone beauty, charm, and confidence, to Karla's surprise and horror, there appeared a roadmap of injustice, lies, and greed, which turned her face into a festering grotesque mask.

In slow motion Karla smashed the mirror with her fist and threw it against the wall. Words from her mouth broke the silence as she screamed, "NO MORE!"

Hebrews 13:5–6 says, "Let your conversation be without covetousness; and be content with such things as ye have: for he hath said, I will never leave thee, nor forsake thee. So that we may boldly say, The Lord is my helper, and I will not fear what man shall do unto me."

Walking into the corporate law offices straight away from the ER with bandaged hand, she held out to her secretary, not an affidavit of complaint sighting willful injustices, but a simple letter of resignation. Immediately she opened her own office and began a plan to make amends and undo the injustices she felt she had incurred in action.

One fine day after several weeks of healing, Karla decided to retrieve that mirror once given to her by her grandmother from behind the bedroom bureau. Reaching far under the dresser she found the mirror's handle and pulled it towards her. As she looked at it, she noticed that of course it was shattered, but all the pieces were in place. Karla knew that she had thrown into the trash pieces of that antique mirror. But how in the world could this be, she wondered? How in the world, indeed? Deep in thought, Karla gently laid it back on the dresser. Something beyond her immediate comprehension was going on.

Remembering a childhood of gentler times, Karla sought out her foundation, Jesus Christ, and looked for a Bible-based church and began to attend, placing before her God instead of greed and the praises of men. Before first light, and every morning, Karla vowed to take a knee, read devotionals, and with God's help, start down a road to recovery.

At first Karla had no clients and was fearful about how she would finance her practice, but keeping it in faith and prayer the Lord delivered. Soon clients were in abundance. Not all had the necessary means for such a high standard of representation, but that was not her concern. Karla's practice flourished, and there was more work than she could handle, and finances were there in place when needed.

One day in a rush Karla returned to her flat, and in the act of getting ready for a court hearing she bumped her hand against the old mirror. Out of curiosity she picked it up, turned it over, and there staring back at her in wonderment was a smiling face without blemish—Karla's youthful glow had returned.

God longs to be our redeemer—He sits waiting for the opportunity. Oddly, Karla did not toss the old mirror into the trash. It stayed where she threw it in wait of retrieval. Do we throw ourselves away thinking that we are too broken to be forgiven and to recover? If we simply, humbly ask, He will hear our cry, deliver us redeemed and made whole again, no matter how broken. The heart of God values our brokenness, and like the pieces of a long-forgotten puzzle He will put our shattered lives back together again for out of our tragedy His glory is made manifest.

No wonder your life, my life, and the world is in calamity. At no other time in history have we been more emotionally wounded, sexually confused, and looking for answers, asking; "Why me? Why is this happening to me?"

Our outcry is in search of the perfect Father and we ask; "What is my value and where is my identity?"

Matthew 3:17 tells us, "This is my beloved Son, in whom I am well pleased." God is eager to answer your cry as well, and bestow in abundance to you more than you can possibly imagine. He promised us in Psalm 2:8, "Ask of Me, and I will give You the nations for Your inheritance, and the ends of the earth for your possession" (NKJV).

Evil has been in existence far longer than this planet has been in existence, and the deceiver knows far more about each and every one of us and what button to push to attain control.

As was said prior, the world comes at us trying to push the breaker and turn us on. Think about Satan tempting Christ. God incarnate, in the flesh, who fasted forty days and nights preparing Himself for ministry surely was feeling hunger pains; the devil knew who Jesus was and he certainly knows who you are. So Satan tried to vex Jesus by casting doubt as he inquired of Jesus, as Matthew 4:3 tells us, "And when the tempter [Satan] came to him, he said, If thou be the Son of God, command that these stones be made bread."

What was Christ's answer? "It is written, Man shall not live by bread alone, but by every word that proceedeth out of the mouth of God" (Matt. 4:4).

Another analogy of a temptation given to Jesus is in Matthew 4:9 where Satan tells Jesus that if Jesus were to worship him, he would give Jesus the world. How might this relate to us today? Imagine that you are standing in the sandals of Jesus, and Satan whispers, "Worship me mortal human … I will give you the world!" This very same enticement hits us every day through television, emails, texts, Facebook, Twitter. Mistress Media beckons us—*give me your precious moments, your money, and I will open the world before you.* Precious moments quickly fleet into hours. Satan has captured your undivided attention … gotcha! What really mattered has wasted away.

Jesus witnessed worldwide misery. He probably saw a mother give birth to a stillborn child and witnessed her heartbreak. He probably saw a farmer plant and toil over the ground just to have nothing grow. Jesus surely witnessed emotional conflagration, hate, anger, war, starvation, needs of the poor, and the ever-growing injustices of that time. Jesus longed to restore the perfection of what once had been the unblemished Eden before sin.

THE MAIN POINT: Matthew 4:8–10 tells us, "Again, the devil took Him [Jesus] up on an exceedingly high mountain, and showed Him all the kingdoms of the world and their glory. And he said to Him, 'All these things I will give You if You will fall down and worship me.' Then Jesus said to him, 'Away with you, Satan! For it is written, "You shall worship the LORD your God, and Him only you shall serve"'" (NKJV).

Christ's heart burst open as He saw and knew what Satan was doing to God's children back then and for the future—human slavery, child sex- trafficking, abortion, prostitution, divorce, war crimes—but He knew what he had to do. Christ stood firm in His conviction and the devil fled. What an example! Jesus must be our gold standard. How much we all long to have the world in our pockets, taking shortcuts to a power career, fame, and adoration, but at what cost? Let us not gain the world and lose our souls over such matters. When push comes to shove, when our still, small voice says, "this is not right," we, too, must have the conviction of our foundation to say, "Get you behind me, Satan!"

Christ took no shortcuts. He drank the bitter cup of suffering and hung on the torturous tree of crucifixion.

Christ took no shortcuts. He drank the bitter cup of suffering and hung on the torturous tree of crucifixion. Christ overcame the world so that we, too, may have the power to do just that. We must also do it God's way and leave self behind. Jesus has given us the power of the Holy Spirit so that by Him and through Him we have total access to God's power in the name of Jesus Christ to create what God has willed us to do—that is, to place God's kingdom government on earth.

While surfing the 300-plus channels of nothing on, I came across a minister delivering a message. He was holding what appeared to be airline tickets in his hand. Upon turning up the volume the question I heard was, "Do you have your ticket friends, brothers, and sisters? You know the plane to heaven is now on the runway and poised for take-off; don't you want to be on board? You don't want to be one of the many who will be left behind!"

He was in the middle of giving the alter call, the invitation to join the soul-saved masses in the name of Jesus Christ. This you could do comfortably seated in your lounger. You would not even have to bother yourself to get up.

Hearing this request almost every Sabbath and hearing about the thousands of baptisms worldwide, of course with the least happening within the USA, I'm a little concerned. After all, there have been thousands of years of missionary work, so why are we not further down salvation road, the path leading to God's intended Kingdom?

The Kingdom Message ...

Matthew 6:33: "But seek ye first the kingdom of God, and his righteousness; and all these things shall be added unto you."

Romans 14:17: "For the kingdom of God is not meat and drink; but righteousness, and peace, and joy in the Holy Ghost."

Gospel preached today is a band-aid. Wars, crime, and devastation we witness today are the result of a gospel that limits itself to preaching a salvation message only.

Hold on there, Hoss! What is wrong with my sermons trying to reach individuals and save their souls one by one? Who do you think you are criticizing the Lord's Good News message? Be careful where you tread!

If I Were the Devil? Back in 1965, a great and wonderful radio commentator during the last three minutes of his broadcast made a very profound closing to that day's dissertation. Paul Harvey stated, "If I Were the Devil..." Then he profoundly and prophetically elaborated on what he would propose. The synopsis was this: If I were the devil, I would keep right on doing what I was doing because the plan was working very well, very well indeed!

If I were the devil, I would not be happy until I seized the ripest apple on the tree—YOU. So I would set about however necessary to

13

subdue and take over the entire planet. First, I'd submit to the churches of these United States with a campaign of whispers; I would whisper to them as I did to Eve

—DO WHATEVER YOU PLEASE. To the young I would whisper that the Bible is a myth. I would convince them that man created God in his image

—instead of the other way around! I would put the belief into the children that what is bad is good and what is good is just no fun and square. And the old I would teach to pray, "OUR FATHER WHO ART IN WASHINGTON…"

Then I'd really get organized. I'd educate authors on how to make normal literature more exciting so that anything else appears dull and uninteresting. I'd threaten TV with dirtier movies and vice versa. I'd peddle narcotics in school yards and wherever I could, and then I'd sell and advertise alcohol to ladies and gentlemen of distinction. I'd tranquilize the rest of the population with pills.

If I were the devil, I'd have families at war with each other … churches at war within themselves … nations at war from within, until each in turn were consumed. And with the promise of higher ratings I'd have the world media fanning the flames of destruction.

If I were the devil, I would encourage schools to refine young intellect but neglect to discipline emotions—just let them run wild until, before you know it, you'd have drug sniffing dogs and metal detectors at every schoolhouse gate.

Soon prisons will overflow. Judges will promote pornography as free speech … now I will evict God from the courthouse, from the school house, and the houses of congress and in God's own churches I will replace religion with psychology, deify science, and lure priests and pastors to misuse and abuse boys and girls with the Lord's tithes and offerings supporting them.

Yes, if I were the devil I'd make the symbol of Easter an egg, the symbol of Christmas a tree accompanied by a celebration with a booze bottle! If I were the devil I'd steal from those who have and give to those who want until I had killed the incentive of the ambitious. What'll ya bet I couldn't get whole states to promote gambling as the way to get rich?????

I would caution against extremes and hard work—patriotism and good moral character! I would convince the young that marriage is just too old- fashioned … that swinging and fooling around is more fun … that what you hear and see on TV is the way to be!

And thus, I, the devil, could undress you in public; I could lure you into bed where there will be diseases for which there are no cures. In other words, if I were the devil—I'd just keep right on doing what he's doing. What do you think?

When the old serpent spied Eve—

He was clever and knew, just how to weave—

The truth of God, into a plan to deceive!

So we sit today on the steps of our sanctuary, head in hand, wondering what are we to do?

It has already been done, my friend. By His resurrection Christ Jesus has taken back title and deed to planet earth with that being the first step to redemption. Heaven is within our grasp.

Are there things in your life that you want to change for the better? When was the last time you put forth an effort to execute a random act of kindness for someone you did not even know? Change must begin within, from the inside out, and what better time than now to start? What would be your first step in doing so?

CHAPTER 2

❧⊶∞⊷❧

Okay, Where Do I Go From Here?

We shall drive out the land grabbers, thieves, squatters, graffiti artists, and all those who have no right to be here. The work of our restoration has begun. Our Savior's mission will return His Father's kingdom to the rightful owner, reclaim it from the enemy, repair what was broken, and place it back to the original intent of creation. God the Father is the rightful King and His heavenly reign shall be restored to earth.

As His sons and daughters, it is our destiny to restore the earth and all the nations in it. This endeavor begins with you and me. Matthew 6:10 reminds us, "Your Kingdom come. Your will be done, On earth as it is in heaven" (NKJV).

This being in our Father's heart a desire for the reality of His kingdom to be manifested on planet earth, a reality of making every activity and condition aligned according to our Father's will. Like an empty glass waiting to be filled, the earth and its inhabitants will receive the rain of righteousness, joy and peace will fall upon us in His kingdom here on earth. We will live by the culture and values of heaven as Jesus instructs us, His disciples, extensively in the ways of His kingdom through scripture.

We must humbly serve one another, having compassion for the sick and less fortunate. We must trust God for all our provisions to carry out

His work of joyfully giving out to others around us who are in need. Choosing the ways of heaven will bring about an abundant life that only God can offer. That which does not exist in heaven should not be allowed in His Kingdom Government on planet Earth.

Returning to My Roots …

Although I grew up in a Christian home back in the 1950s and 1960s, when the call of the wild world caused me to pick up the curriculum of rock n' roll, I was off to the races. But in 1983 that idea came to an abrupt halt, as it felt good to stop beating my head against a wall of dreams that would never come true.

Then in the late 1990s, the tempo of life picked up beat and my wife and I were living a great and comfortable, worldly life. At the time we did not know of the grace and goodness of the Lord Jesus very well … like many we were just too busy, and besides that, we were financially blessed; we did not need any help, or so we thought. We could do whatever, whenever, we wanted. Nice vacations were on life's menu and we took advantage of it. Then, one day after returning from an over-the-holidays, month-long vacation, something happened. Ooops!

Business-wise things were not the same as when we had left. The daily operations of the company were to be left in the hands of certain trusted caretakers while we were traveling. Suddenly these individuals desired to be us. "Nest-feathering," as you might call it, had been going on behind our backs. Hey, it is tough being me, but to now have someone else sharing my shoes made it difficult to stand.

Shrouded within a veil of lies and excuses they left our company behind and went to another town close by, to cookie-cutter what we were doing, taking along with them contacts and customers who were once part of our stable. Such is the way of the world—one day you are all in and the next you are standing with an entirely different view of things.

What do you mean you are now buying from so and so? "Well, he said you were retiring and leaving all your business decisions to him," was the customer's reply.

With handwriting clearly on the wall I had to make some business maneuvers. Only now I had to do it with just part of my income to pay bills, and with the full onslaught of debt per month, we were in trouble. But hey, I got this covered, just tweak it here, adjust there ... but check and check and there laughing, taunting me was the face of check-mate looming on the horizon.

It was time for the situation room and an alternate plan. My parents were living with us in an in-law's quarters. We had at the time, along with mom and dad, a family of five, three warehouses, two stores, and a mountain of leased obligations plus the usual monthly debt. A Bible verse came to my mind: you have been weighed and you are found wanting (Dan. 5:27)! I called my accountant for advice ... "File bankruptcy, Larry," was their recommendation. I did not know it at the time, but it was not finances that were wanting, but rather it was my soul that was being weighed and bargained for. Hhhhmmm?

Let's consider the story of Job. Remember that in this life Satan has the right to attack and trouble us by whatever means are at his disposal. Our troubles are not the signs of punishment, as generally considered by many, caused by our wrongdoings or caused by those of our parent's history. It is true, however, that it is because of the original transgression of God's law that sin exists in the world. But the truth of the matter has become distorted. Satan, the author of lies, sin, and the result of it, led men to believe that disease and death proceeded from God as punishment arbitrarily inflicted upon man because of sin. So therefore, those upon whom some great calamity falls have not just that burden, but also the black eye of being regarded as an example of what happens to you when you sin. The history of Job shows that our suffering is inflicted by Satan but is overruled by God for the purpose of mercy. Also realize that after we find mercy it is by our choice that we revisit the same path that led us to sorrow. We choose the paths we walk; one is the narrow road of the righteous and the other is the wide, spiraling road to perdition.

One day melted into another until the stress was about to topple my already leaning spiritual tower.

One day melted into another until the stress was about to topple my already leaning spiritual tower. It was early one day, and I chose to go it alone to my office. I walked into the cold, dark warehouse and didn't bother to turn on the lights as I made my way to the office. Before going in I turned around and shouted at the darkness, "What do you want from me? What do you want me to do about this mess?"

Entering the office, I turned on the lights and sat down at my desk. A stack of bills and my check ledger stared back at me from where I had left them idle at the close of business the day before. *Nothing new under the sun,* I thought.

Mulling over the situation my mind drifted to thoughts of my childhood. Boy were they happier times! I remembered childhood friends and the old village church came to mind. We used to walk there—Mom, Grandma, my brother, and I just about every Sunday. I was baptized in that old white clap- boarded structure when I was twelve. Funny the things that suddenly surface to memory, huh? Tears of melancholy appeared and ran down my cheeks; pictures of Mom, Dad, Grandma, and my younger brother ... the baptism, Reverend Wright who always asked Mom how I was doing, my mom always telling me that she will always pray for me ... gee-wiz, how much more could I take?

Like an ice bullet striking me between the eyes, it was so simple, so obvious ... one never stands so tall as when one drops to their knees, humbles before the cross, calls upon the Lord in the name of Jesus Christ, and confesses, "What a fool I've been! Lord, You have been here all the time tapping me on the shoulder as I ran in the opposite direction. You would call out to my deaf ears asking, 'What about Me? Have you called upon Me lately for help?'" Keep your life free from the concerns of money, and be content with what you have, for He has said, "I will never leave you or abandon you" (Heb. 13:5).

That was the final factor. Once again I turned my life completely—lock, stock, barrel, business, and family—over to the Lord. Best move I ever made. No, I was not filing bankruptcy and hurting a lot of people in the process; I placed all my concerns into the capable hands of the Lord, and together we would swim out of this was His blessed assurance.

Arriving home that evening, as soon as I walked through the door, right on time the phone rang. I picked up the call and it was a colleague telling me he was on the way back from a Texas business trip. He explained that he and his partner were opening a warehouse in Texas and were looking for two expert people to run the business. I asked if he would consider me and he laughed, "What, with all that you have going on?"

My reply was, "You have no idea what is going on."

It was mid-November and he said, "If you can be there by January 1st you have a deal, but your wife must be our warehouse manager and you will oversee the operation."

"Done," was my reply without hesitation.

Hanging up the phone I looked at my wife and she at me and she asked, "Where's Texas and is it any warmer than the northeast?"

"Yup, pard' it's a mite south of here and is definitely a little bit warmer," I said, assuring her with a smile.

At that same time in our relationship my wife had been attending a Bible- based, Sabbath-keeping church and had been telling me that when we did go to church on Sunday we did not worship on the correct day. I said that it did not matter on what day we worshiped, just so it was at least one day a week; God would be pleased with the effort. So I set out and started studying the Bible, Genesis to Revelation, surfed the internet gathering historical Biblical background, arming myself in readiness just to prove her wrong. (*More about the outcome of that study later* …)

Aside from that endeavor, for the moment several things had to happen in order to bring closure to our present position. Leases had to be transferred or bought out, warehouses and stores closed or sold, and our home property had to be listed for sale. All had to happen in less than two months. Who did I call upon to accomplish these tasks? I will give you several clues—it was not my accountant, not a real estate agent, not a banker or attorney. Yes, you guessed it. Falling to my knees I called upon the greatest Hero ever to visit planet earth: Jesus Christ.

The whole process was watching a true-to-life miracle take place as all the pieces to the puzzle fell into position. You can't make this stuff up and truth is far greater than fiction. The house sold for above market, one store was sold, the other closed, and leases were taken up by other parties. One by one the financial burdens abated, allowing us to move forward.

Arrival in Texas was on schedule for me, but I had to leave my dear wife back east to clear up and clean up all the loose ends. As I said the house was sold and our real estate agent had made good on her promise, too: "I will have the house sold by the end of the year." *Really*, I thought at first, *no way*, but it did happen ... oh, me of little faith. It was to close the day before the closing of the house we purchased with a bridge loan in Texas. The transfer of that money from the sale of the home in Pennsylvania would pay off the bridge loan, thus taking care of the down payment on the new house in Texas. The monetary dominos would fall into place and we were good to go. I was on top of the world. With a smile on my lips and surety in my steps I went on with life and business as usual until at mid-morning on the day of the closing of our home in Pennsylvania. My cell phone vibrated and then a ring sounded out ... or was that the noise of screeching brakes as my "Happy Train" derailed, crashing into the unknown abyss of despair.

"Whud'ya mean the sale is not closed?" was my question to the real estate agent on the other end of the call. "Whud'ya mean the husband refuses to sign the loan documents?"

Explanation: "He claims that his wife went ahead without him on all of this even though he signed (p. p., *per procurationem*) the preliminary sales agreements. He said that he wanted to see the property first before signing the final sales agreement and that did not happen, so he is hesitating at this point."

I was silent and then the agent asked, "Are you there, Larry? Did you hear me?"

"Do you know what is at stake here?" I asked.

"Yes, and don't worry," was her reply, "They can't back out of this now. I know these people personally and I will apply pressure ... just give me some time to work on them."

Our furniture was being moved into the new home as we were speaking. I had been living there for over a month on a futon and take-out, and as I placed the cell phone back in its holster, I stood staring blankly in disbelief. Retracing my life over the last month-and-a-half I figured it out and I made a call ... it was not to my accountant, not to the real estate agent, not a banker or attorney. You guessed who it was, didn't you? You see, I realized that in all of this busyness I had not included the very One person who made this all possible—my good Lord and Savior, Jesus Christ. So what did I do? I made the call, dropped to my knees, and got on the direct line to heaven. After the call I stood up smiling, knowing that everything was under control.

Looking at me like I had just sprouted two heads, my wife asked, "What in the world are you smiling about? All this terrible drama is unfolding— what are we going to do?"

My reply, "Nothing, Claudia. The Lord's got this. Everything will be okay."

"Okay, if you say so," she said and added, "I wish that I had your faith."

Hours passed as we filled our time with putting things from the moving van in place. Occasionally I looked at my watch and then I would look upward as I remembered, "The Lord's got this." The morning quickly merged into afternoon and afternoon into early evening. Again I checked the time and looked heavenward.

Waking me from my skyward daze the cell phone rang out and I quickly answered, recognizing the number.

"Hello," I answered in breathless anticipation. At first there was a pregnant pause. Then silence gave birth to dialogue which was almost a whisper, "Ye of little faith. I told you I would get this done and the money you require is at this moment being transferred to the bank of your closing."

"But how is this possible?" I asked. "I thought the deal was scuttled?"

"I threatened to sue them for breach of contract," was the agent's reply ending with a laugh. "Besides, he was my cousin who was waffling on the matter, and he knows I am serious about what I say I will do."

"The Lord works in mysterious ways His wonders to perform," I said with a smile and gave the agent a hearty "thank-you" and much appreciation for her efforts.

After hanging up the phone my wife and I took time and gave thanks to the One who deserves all our accolades of gladness and appreciation. Amen.

The point of this story is to have you make a consideration. Place God first. No self-proclaiming Christian would deny that Christ is first in everything they do. "These people ... honor Me with their lips, but their heart is far from Me" (Matthew 15:8, NKJV).

What does your life's story tell you as you reflect as I did on the past few months after moving to Texas?

If it is our desire to be part of God's kingdom, then we must realize that it's all about Him.

If it is our desire to be part of God's kingdom, then we must realize that it's all about Him.

Revelation 2:4 says, "But I have this against you, that you have abandoned the love you had at first" (ESV). And in Ecclesiastes 7:29 we read, "Lo, this only have I found, that God hath made man upright; but they have sought out many inventions."

You see, just as God created Adam and Eve and made them free moral agents, we, too, are wonderfully made in that regard. In our hearts we are capable of appreciating the wisdom and benevolence of His character and also the justice of His requirements and expectations. Thus, since we are not robots, we can withhold obedience. Just as our parents of Eden were considered for eternal security, loyalty had to be found, a check on self- indulgence tested. Self-indulgence lay at the foundation of Satan's fall. It is our fatal passion, *fait accompli,* but when asked, God will intercede with *coup de grace* to end our worldly struggle so that we might shed these earthly pleasures of the flesh. As we are exposed to Satan's temptations, we must remain steadfast and endure this trial, for one day we will be placed beyond his power and influence to enjoy God's perpetual favor and influence. "Because sentence against an evil work is not executed speedily, therefore the heart of the sons of men is fully set in them to do evil" (Eccles. 8:11).

A dear friend of mine who was an attorney once told me, "The wheels of law move slowly but grind very fine the justice to be meted out." So, from God man tries to mirror this way of measuring out justice, perhaps. God uses His intended agents to call all to allegiance and offers a full pardon if they will repent. But for the very reason that God is long suffering, men presume God's mercy. This love should soften men's hearts, but it has an entirely different affect against the careless and sinful, as it only strengthens their resistance. If we would live in an instantaneous retributive state, offenses against God would not rage rampant and unchecked. However, delayed punishment is certain. There are limits even within God's mercy. Once God does take up the case of the presumptuous, He will not cease until all sin is put to an end.

So as it is in God's heavenly kingdom, sin will not stand in His earthly government, either. (Remember: On earth as it is in heaven…) Darkness as sin and light as righteousness cannot occupy the same space.

You may be thinking, "Hhhmm, I need to put God first in my life." How can you do that if He is not even third or fourth? By careful examination would it be problematic to give it all over to God—yourself, your family, your business or job, everything? You see, it is not you who chooses as He has already chosen you and it is all because of John 3:16, "For God so loved the world that He gave His only begotten Son, that whosoever believeth in Him shall not perish, but have everlasting life."

It's a gift and all you have to do is accept it.

Jesus said in John 15:5, "I am the vine, you are the branches; he who abides in Me and I in him, bears much fruit; for without Me you can do nothing" (NKJV). And in John 15:16 Jesus says, "You did not choose Me, but I chose you and appointed you that you should go and bear fruit, and that your fruit should remain, that whatever you ask the Father in my name He may give you.

As we said before, Christ died so that we may live in His Father's Kingdom. By repentance through trusting Christ alone for our salvation we have been saved. God no longer sees our sin, but sees instead the perfection of Christ.

2 Corinthians 5:17–20 says, "Therefore, if anyone is in Christ, he is a new creation. The old has passed away; behold, the new has come. All this is from God, who through Christ reconciled us to himself and gave us the ministry of reconciliation; that is, in Christ God was reconciling the world to himself, not counting their trespasses against them, and entrusting to us the message of reconciliation. Therefore, we are ambassadors for Christ, God making his appeal through us. We implore you on behalf of Christ, be reconciled to God" (ESV),

Matthew 28:19–20 implores us, "Go ye therefore, and teach [make] all nations, baptizing them in the name of the Father, and of the Son, and of the Holy Ghost: Teaching them to observe all things whatsoever I have commanded you: and, lo, I am with you always, even unto the end of the world. Amen."

Chapter 3

Back to the Future and Its Benefits

It has been said that you can't know where you are going until you know where you've been. As stated previously, our parents of Eden made an error which catapulted not only themselves but all future generations into a theatre of great controversy. That was then, and we are still on stage playing out this insane act in an attempt to undo what was done by making the wrong choice and disobeying God's command. However, we as human flesh are not capable of going it alone. Our hope is that by recognizing our weakness we can be made perfect again through our choice of reconciliation through Jesus Christ.

Let's review our original creation in Genesis 1:26–28: "And God said, Let **us** make man in **our** image [Note: *US* not *me*], <u>after **our** likeness</u> [we are talking about the character of God here]: and let them have **DOMINION** over the fish of the sea, and over the fowl of the air, and over the cattle, and over all the earth, and over every creeping thing that creepeth upon the earth. So God created man in His own image, in the image of God created he him; male and female created he them. And God blessed them, and God said unto them, Be fruitful, and multiply, and replenish the earth, and subdue it: and have **dominion** over the fish of the sea, and over the fowl of the air, and over every living thing that moveth upon the earth" (emphasis added).

I bolded **dominion** for a reason; the Hebrew word is **Radah** and it is a royal word—a "God's Kingdom" word, if you will. In Psalm 72, "*A Psalm for Solomon,*" in verses 8 and also 12–14 we see what God wanted for and from the wisest man on the planet. "He shall have **dominion** also from sea to sea, and from the river unto the ends of the earth ... For he shall deliver the needy when he crieth; the poor also, and him that hath no helper. He shall spare the poor and needy, and shall save the souls of the needy. He shall redeem their soul from deceit and violence and precious shall their blood be in his sight."

What God desires in His kingdom is a societal climate where the defenseless are protected and one that gives justice to the oppressed. In Ezekiel 34:7–8, God sends a strong message via the prophet, reprimanding the kings of that day for their disobedience and wickedness. "Therefore, ye shepherds [kings], hear the word of the LORD; As I live, saith the LORD GOD, surely because my flock became a prey, and my flock became meat to every beast of the field, because there was no shepherd, neither did my shepherds search for my flock, but the shepherds fed themselves, and fed not my flock." The Lord goes on to say that He will be taking back His gifts and the situation, and that their rule no longer stands, and those kings will instead find themselves wanting.

I found a beautiful paraphrase of Genesis 1:28: *"Be fruitful and have children filling the earth with your life so that you can have power to fight against everything that leads to death. Rule with care and fairness over the natural world, over the myriads of my beautiful creatures—from tropical fish to soaring eagles to dogs and cats—every creature that is a part of this living world"* (author unknown).

God's intent was that we are to be ambassadors on planet earth—an extension of the kingdom of heaven. God specifically made the world to enlarge His heavenly influence. He desires a larger family of created intelligences. "All heaven took a deep and joyful interest in the creation of the world and of man. Human beings were a new and distinct order. They were wonderfully made *"in the image of God,"* and it was the Creator's desire and design that they should populate the earth. (White, "Purpose of Man's Creation," *Review and Herald,* Feb. 11, 1902)

27

When you trust in Christ and begin to more and more take on God's intended character, you become a light to a dark world. You will begin to reflect the life of Christ and submit to the will of God the Father. When you put God first, you spend time in prayer, serve others, and think of yourself less often. Soon you will say, "Not my will, but Your will Lord; not my glory, but for Your glory Lord.: The things you are willing to do in His name are for the advancement of God's kingdom on earth. You will begin to bear the burdens of others and make sacrifices. Of course, you will not be perfect, but the synergy of your life will change day by day.

Apostle Paul said in 1 Corinthians 11:1, "Follow my example, as I follow the example of Christ" (NIV). He also says in Galatians 2:20, "I have been crucified with Christ; it is no longer I who live, but Christ lives in me; and the life which I now live in the flesh I live by faith in the Son of God, who loved me and gave himself for me" (NKJV).

And notably in 1 John 1:7 we are assured, "But if we walk in the light, as he [Jesus] is in the light, we have fellowship with one another, and the blood of Jesus, His [God's] Son, purifies us from all sin" (NIV).

There are so many distractions in this world today and the bling of it seeks to slow our work in progress towards a higher calling. Many will challenge, "Well, go ahead—show me. If I could only catch a glimpse of heaven's glory, I would immediately change my whole lifestyle." What are you as a believer going to tell someone if they ask you that question? The best response is your testimony and your story—the before and now and what lies ahead in your future.

The wonderful benefits don't just **poof** and happen overnight. How long did it take you—how long has it taken society—to reach the dilemma we are in today? It has been going on for millennia. Be wise in your use of time, readjust your mindset to a more devotional prayer life, and set priorities; let your horizon be to a higher calling by helping others and allow God to be your center point in every decision.

What gifts do you have? Use them for His glory and through Him you will help to advance God's kingdom on earth. Glorify God in all you do and prayerfully ask for a better understanding of Jesus and the scriptures, and to trust the Lord in all things. By faith and trusting in Him, allow God to lead you.

We exist in brokenness … our immediate environment, our nation, moves about in a moral fog within a spiritual twilight. Our life has been spin- doctored; immorality modified, dishonesty modified, sophistry and denial are business as usual. But by faith in the leadership of Jesus Christ we will restore ourselves, our nation, and prepare the world.

As people, as a church, we cannot simply make our mission to evangelize individuals one-by-one as the norm. Don't take this the wrong way; of course it is good to witness wherever and whenever possible. Of course it is good to bring souls to Christ. But we must consider God's original plan of making a difference to change the overall societal climate within an entire country and bring forward the concept of God's kingdom on planet earth.

Ephesians 6:12 tells us, "For we wrestle not against the flesh and blood, but against principalities, against powers, against the rulers of the darkness of this world, against spiritual wickedness in high places."

Just as in apostle Paul's time, it is even truer today. We look about in disbelief at the atrocities which are being carried out right before our eyes.

One day back in the 60s I was sitting on a doorstep in Long Beach, California, and I was handing out literature claiming that the system— our government and its leaders in charge, yes even way back then—were corrupt and Washington needed a good house cleaning from the top down. Later that did happen as more and more evidence was brought to light.

However, that day was hot and I was tired of standing on the corner, so I bought some water from a local store and sat down. A door opened behind me and there appeared a well-dressed man who I later found out through conversation was an attorney and the stoop I was holding down was the entrance to a law practice. He was nice about it and told me not to get up and he politely sat down beside me.

29

The attorney took one of my pamphlets and read the front page and smiled and asked, "Do you think that '*Tricky Dick*' is the only one that should be indicted for treasonous acts?"

"I don't know," was my reply.

"Of course you don't, and no one will ever know the whole truth behind the agenda of a shadowed government. But I predict that he will take the fall to end the matter," the attorney said then added, "You've got guts to stand out here and hand out flyers on such a hot topic about a controversial war in which so many innocents have died. But let me tell you something. Do the research on what you are selling. Don't do it just because this radical idea is in vogue and you feel it is the thing to do—believe it and own it. You will be more convincing that way and if you really want to make a difference do what I did."

"What's that?" I asked as the attorney handed me a card with a smile. "Cut your hair to an acceptable length, get an education, and fight for change from within. Then they will believe you are one of them. Be a chameleon and before you know it you will be running your own small show which will lead you onto a broader influential stage," the attorney suggested, holding out his hand.

Shaking his hand without looking at the card I asked, "What's your name?"

"Cochran," the man said, "Attorney Cochran. My friends call me Johnny, and if I can be of any help in any way, shape, or form, call that number; let me know, okay?"

I never saw the man again and I continued going my own way but the point I took from that brief conversation was that we must prepare for whatever endeavor we are taking on, to the very best of our ability. If it is our intent to prepare the world at large for the heavenly kingdom on planet earth, let us take up the cross as God's stewards.

The preaching of the gospel of salvation has produced Christians, but so far as the understanding of the gospel of the kingdom, it has yet to be understood as to how it applies to us individually, and even more how it relates to us as a nation and our culture. This applies to all nations covering the entire world as God has given every church a greater vision to disciple nations. When the body of Christ begins to understand this, they will actively engage with societal issues and pray and speak up against legalized gambling, prostitution, and the redefinition of marriage. Our heavenly assignments include the strengthening of our nation's economy and community development projects that are of benefit to all people. We must make the discipleship of not just our nation, but nations worldwide.

Christians who love their country want more than just a higher percentage of converts; it should be a goal of a clean government promoting a prosperous economy and caring communities where the needy are taken care of.

This radical new way of thinking embraced by Jesus Christ is an invitation for His Christian body of believers to become more involved in the world and surrender the excuse that "this is not our home; we belong to heaven." We now should embrace the truth that while heaven is our destination, to have dominion over the earth is our destiny.

I grew up in the green pastures of sweet home Pennsylvania within a cultural bubble. However, I was swayed by the influence of the 60s revolution and rock and roll. Being a musician, I traveled all over in that line of work until 1983. It has been suggested that we as Christians stay away from the music business, as well as from acting and professional sports. It has even been suggested to steer clear from a career in business as the influence of money will corrupt and bring about the power that is absolutely corruptible.

By condemning these areas of society as being unredeemable, we have unknowingly handed them over to the enemy without a fight—sine pugna.

Psalm 2:8 says, "Ask of me, and I shall give thee the heathen for thine inheritance, and the uttermost parts of the earth for thy possession."

In our time there are the brave; our sons and daughters are being called out by God. Fearless they are shining their light into the darkest recesses of perverted industries, calling them out for what they are, identifying and labeling them and holding responsible parties accountable.

This is for God's sons and daughters a daunting task, but be not afraid. Romans 8:14 promises, "For as many as are led by the Spirit of God, they are the sons of God." 1 Corinthians 6:15 also tells us, "Know ye not that your bodies are the members of Christ? Shall I then take the members of Christ and make them the members of a harlot? God forbid."

The nations are the inheritance that God promised to His Son, Jesus. Being saved by Jesus we are adopted into His family as children of God and are entitled to His inheritance. "But if the spirit of Him that raised up Jesus from the dead dwell in you, he that raised up Christ from the dead shall also quicken your mortal bodies by his Spirit that dwelleth in you" (Rom. 8:11). 1 Corinthians 6:14 goes on to say, "And God hath both raised up the Lord, and will also raise up us by his own power."

These are encouraging words and victory will be ours if we believe it. Every victory is a gem in the crown of life. The Christian is a spectacle to the world, to angels, and to men. Singular? Yes—he has a singular, most peculiar character because his life is worked out by a nature similar to divinity.

Inhabitants of unfallen worlds and of the heavenly universe are watching with intense interest the conflict between good and evil. They rejoice as Satan's subtleties, one after another, are discerned and met with, "**It is written,**" just as Christ met them in His conflict with the wily foe. Every victory we claim on the Lord's behalf is a gem in the crown of life. In the day of victory all the universe of heaven triumphs. The harps of the angels send forth the most beautiful music, accompanying the melody of voice. Hallelujah!

According to Matthew 4:3–4, "And when the tempter came to Him, he said, If thou be the Son of God, command that these stones be made bread. But He [Jesus] answered and said, **It is written**, Man shall not live by bread alone, but by every word that proceedeth out of the mouth of God" (emphasis added).

We must finish the work and meet it head on as God had requested in Exodus 19:6. "And ye shall be unto me a kingdom of priests, and an holy nation. These are the words which thou shall speak unto the children of Israel." God was speaking to Moses here. Today God is speaking to us. Israel was God's chosen physical nation and people who were sent a commission and they did not deliver on the promise. Today we are, simply put, the new Spiritual Israel, commissioned by God to finish the work.

Who are we to take up the cross and finish the work? How do we claim access? Hear us, O Lord, we who were once broken. We will now bring healing to broken families and communities. We who were once sin-driven and mad with passion will now become passionate about purity and establish His goodness in the corrupt systems and governments. We who were unjust will now establish and display justice to the oppressed. We who were once the unloved will now express God's redeeming love to transform the kingdoms of this world.

The Triumph of God is in Revelations 11:15: "And the seventh angel sounded; and there were great voices in heaven, saying, The kingdoms of this world are become the kingdoms of our Lord, and of his Christ; and he shall reign for ever and ever."

CHAPTER 4

Healthy Body, Healthy Mind, Healthy Spirit

Perilous pathways to discovery of truth are just this: *a razor's edge.* While endeavoring to go through many phases and much soul searching, each of us in our own way, at different stages of life, attempt to make sense of it all. Giving my life over to Jesus Christ forty-plus years ago, I set out on what was intended to be an honorable and diligent quest. I am, and will always be, I confess, a *"WIP"*—Work in Progress. That is where the journey started for me and much unrealized work began. Truth is found within one's self; a contractual obligation and partnership based on love, understanding, and forgiveness. All life's journeys are different, and each individual has to work out that which is peculiar to their own situation. Within me darkness still abides and holds court. In those areas I need to seek the Light of Truth and sweep away the cobwebs of doubt in order to set my spirit free in Jesus Christ. There can be no proclaiming salvation until I confess all my transgressions to God.

Truth is found within one's self; a contractual obligation and partnership based on love, understanding, and forgiveness.

As humans we are interwoven with naivety, innocence, worldly experience, historical fact, personal observation, falling down and getting up, and moving in and out of grace. We think at times we have left the Lord behind, but within my reality, when I look back and see only one set of footprints in the sand, that was when the good Lord was carrying me. I believed on my journey that at numerous times I had done just that—left Him behind—only to feel the good Lord tapping me on the shoulder asking, "Remember me?"

My erroneous reply, "Soon Lord … I'll get back to You real soon on that.

I'm kinda busy right now."

Compelling change in our lives brings about progress. You will never adventure to lose sight of the sea of doubt unless you dip your toes in the water, dive in, and swim about in the pool of change and take life on faith. Shed off the chains that bind you. You have the keys; there is the gift box of grace and forgiveness—accept and open it. The power of freedom is within your grasp.

A man on a mat sat beside the pool of Bethesda in Jerusalem waiting for the angel of the Lord to come down and trouble the water.

Trouble is the key word here. Oh, how our troubles bring about the intervention of change. At times it is whatever moves you forward and pushes you back … but let's see what scripture says.

The man was bound to his mat and his paralytic disease for over thirty years. He claimed no one would help him to get into the pool so he could be healed. He watched as time after time people would get into the water ahead of him and claim the victory. *Woe is me* he would think, "I'm too weak." "I am too old." "I am too ugly." "I am too bold." "I am too tired." "I am too busy." "People ignore me." "It is too late for me." "It's too early." "I am too fat." "I am too skinny." "Help me somebody please!" The list grew (grows) daily as he (we) turned them over and over in his (our) troubled mind.

Suddenly a voice like that of an angel said to him, "Do you want to be healed?" The man hesitated, and instead of replying with,

"HALLELUJAH! YES—PRAISE JESUS, I WANT TO BE HEALED!" he unpacked his laundry list of shortcomings and grievances!

Gently, the voice requested, "Pick up your mat and walk." Jesus met the man as he was. The gift of grace was delivered.

Accepting the gift, the man did as asked.

As the man picked up his mat and walked away it showed that he carried his burden with him, but he received the blessing, grasped hold of the gift, mustered the courage to get off the mat, and moved on in faith. We all carry baggage just as he did, but we must make the move, go forward to make a new beginning. If we don't, we will remain on the mat paralytic— spiritually, physically, mentally, addicted to the paralysis that binds us. So when trouble stirs the waters of your life, pick up the mat you are sitting on and start walking. Claim the victory! We are all of us a glorious work in progress for the greater good.

It is a question of balance. God wants us to be healthy in all areas: body, mind, and spirit. By God's original intent we are wonderfully made. Psalms 139:14 says, "I will praise thee; for I am fearfully and wonderfully made: marvellous are thy works; and that my soul knowest right well."

The Power of Debased Appetite: "All was lost when Adam yielded to the power of appetite. The Redeemer, in whom was united both the human and the divine, stood in Adam's place, and endured a terrible fast of nearly six weeks. The length of this fast is the strongest evidence of the extent of the sinfulness and the power of debased appetite upon the human family" (White, *Selected Messages,* vol. 1, p. 272).

A Lesson to Take to Ourselves: "Christ was our example in all things. As we see his humiliation in the long trial and fast in the wilderness to overcome the temptations of appetite in our behalf, we are to take this lesson home to ourselves when we are tempted. If the power of appetite is so strong upon the human family, and its indulgence so fearful that the Son of God subjected himself to such a test, how important that we should feel the necessity to have appetite under the control of reason. Our savior lasted nearly six weeks so that he might gain for man the victory upon the point of appetite. How can professed Christians with an enlightened conscious, and Christ before them a pattern, yield to the indulgence of appetites which have an enervating influence upon the mind and heart? It is a painful fact that habits of self-gratification at the expense of health, and the weakening of moral power, are holding us in the bonds of slavery at the present time in a large share of the Christian world" (White, *SDA Bible Commentary, vol. 5,* p.1079).

Back in the 60s there was a song written titled "Woodstock" by a folk singer named Joni Mitchell. I bring this up because I am of that generation

—I was a musician and at that time a vegetarian before it became in vogue. People did not think about organics as they do now, and did not consider the healthy lifestyles that are today looked upon something to be achieved. Yes, I was a traveling musician hippie-type, just as the fellows who founded Whole Foods (the widespread organic grocery chain) were of the flower child generation. And as a matter of fact, I used Dr. Bronner's Organic Castile Soap® products way back then because you could shower, shave, and even brush your teeth with it in cold or hot water. So how about that all you who think you have discovered something unique and special for the first time? Well ho, ho, ho—what do you know? You are now just playing catch-up. And out of that generation came the fortitude to stand up and protest and say we are mad as everything and we are not going to take it anymore!

Oh yes, the song "Woodstock" … It has some interesting lyrics. The singer mentions that we are stardust and are tied up in Satan's contract and we have to once again find Eden.

Hhhmm … from a hippie-chick, folk singer no less. What was she thinking?

Back to "the garden" (that being Eden) which was a copy of heaven, by the way … and right here on planet earth, too. "God created man in his own image … male and female created he them" (Gen. 1:27).

Here in this garden called Eden is set forth the origin of the human race; and the origin of the human race is so plainly stated that there is no occasion to jump to erroneous conclusions. "God created man in His own image." Where, dear brother and sister, is the great mystery and where lies the sinking sand of supposition that man evolved by slow degrees of development from lower life forms and decaying plant matter? The sinking sand is the theory of the evolutionists who have lowered the work of the divine Creator to the level of man's narrow, earthly conceptions. Men are so bent upon excluding God from the sovereignty of the universe that they unwittingly have degraded themselves and all mankind, defrauding the world of the dignity of its origin.

The genealogy of our race, as given by divine inspiration, traces back its origin, not to a line of developing germs, nematodes, and quadrupeds, but to the great Creator. Though formed from the dust of the earth, Adam was "the son of God."

Don't worry sisters—you are included in this divine work as well, because God Himself gave Adam a personal companion, one who could be with him in love and sympathy. In order to do this God gently put Adam to sleep and took from Adam one of his ribs, signifying that she was not to control him as the head, nor to be trampled under his foot as inferior either. Eve was to stand by Adam's side as equal, to be loved and protected by him. She was part of man, bone of his bone and flesh of his flesh. She was his second self, showing the close union and the affectionate attachment that should exist in this relationship. "For no man ever yet hated his own flesh; but nourisheth it and cherisheth it" (Eph. 5:29). And also, "Therefore shall a man leave his father and his mother, and shall cleave unto his wife: and they shall be one flesh" (Gen.2:24).

In this act of creation God celebrated the first marriage. This institution has for its originator the Creator of the universe. "Marriage is honourable" (Heb. 13:4); it was one of the first gifts of God to man, and it is one of the two institutions that Adam brought with him after the fall, beyond the gates of Paradise.

When the divine principles are recognized and obeyed in the relationship of marriage, it is a blessing. However, today this blessed truth is not followed. With political correctness creeping in it has morphed into an abomination. Marriage as a blessing. It guards the purity and the happiness of the race; it provides for man's social needs; it elevates the physical, the intellectual, and most of all, our moral nature.

We are designed for a special task. In every stage of this earth's history God has had His agencies to carry forward His work, which must be done in an appointed way. John the Baptist was one of those. When the angel Gabriel approached Zacharias telling him that his wife Elisabeth, who was barren and beyond child birthing capabilities because of age, would give him a son, he had doubt. The angel told Zacharias the plan: no wine or strong drink for the boy who shall be named John and he shall be filled with the Holy Ghost even from his mother's womb. And many of the children of Israel shall be turned to the Lord their God because of him (Luke 1:16). Because of his doubt Zechariahs was struck dumb until the birth of John. "For as many as are led by the Spirit of God, they are the sons of God" (Rom. 8:14).

John is an example of the saying, "We are what we eat." Even today we must remember God's desire for our physical health. "Beloved, I wish above all things that thou mayest prosper and be in health, even as thy soul prospereth" (3 John 2). I will also add Proverbs 23:7: "For as he thinketh in his heart, so is he." Now more than ever we must be cautious as to what we allow into our heart; what we watch, listen to, read, and especially what we put into our mouths. It is not like the good old days of my youth growing up on a farm. There we fed our chickens and they were free range. We knew the names of the cows that grazed on its grass; they were fed corn from the farm and they provided us milk, butter, and cheese, and we knew the ones that would be later processed. It was a different time and we were predominately self-sufficient. We had our own well for drinking water, springs were used for irrigation, and we ate our own fruits and vegetables.

This is not the average normal American lifestyle today, and my father told me that during the Great Depression, in those times of great monetary conflagration, he was very fortunate. "I was glad to be a poor dirt farmer," he said, "living off the land having less than two plug nickels to rub together rather than have to fight it out as a hobo riding the rails, scratching for a few dollars, or be sleeping on the street, penniless."

How far we have come from the days of my father and the old farm lifestyle! But we must ask, "What have we lost?" No longer do we absolutely know where our food comes from. Can we really trust what they say it is? Farm fresh? Free range? Organic? What are the facts? What are our government's stipulations to qualify for such a label?

By eating and drinking all the processed foods and drinks that come our way via convenience, we short-sell ourselves body, mind, and spirit. If you drink too many alcoholic beverages, what happens? You become drunk and quickly your mental and physical processes are numbed, and reason is compromised. The same thing happens as we put into our body processed foods, but the degradation of our body is not readily visible. Eventually the lack of essential vitamins and minerals leads to a slow death of all cells bringing on physical impairment, diminishing mental acuity.

We have all heard the story, if not seen the video documentary, about the man who subjected himself to a whole month of eating a well-known purveyor of fast food's super-sized meals. First, he was examined by his physician as being in reasonably good health and at the end of those thirty days he returned for a reexamination and was found to be on death's door.

That was extreme, but for all of us, instead, think of this act as being slowed down, with the end result being just as sure. Without realizing it, the choices we make every day by what we eat and drink change our bodies either to nourish or impinge its functional process. More fruits and veggies, more glasses of distilled water, two meals rather than three, no snacks unless it is fruits, nuts, or veggies, less or no salt, less sugar, less processed foods in general, only organics, no dairy, no eggs … BUT if ya just gotta eat meat and dairy, make it free-range, organic please. Hey, we are all a work in progress, but the point is cast your vote at the checkout and get started. Tell these mega corporations we mean business and hurt them where it counts—in their wallets.

There are other ways to eat healthy aside from the main-line grocery stores and help others as well. If you live near a rural community, look for local farm markets and when shopping there ask them questions. Are you organic growers, and if not, where do you get your fruits and vegetables, eggs, honey, etc.?

1 Corinthians 6:19–20 says, "What? Know ye not that your body is the temple of the Holy Ghost which is in you, which ye have of God, and ye are not your own? For ye are bought with a price: therefore glorify God in your body, and in your spirit, which are God's." Paul also goes on to tell us in 1 Corinthians 10:31, "Whether therefore ye eat, or drink, or whatsoever you do, do all to the glory of God."

Let me ask you a question. Imagine a bright, sunshiny day, with a cloudless sky, the temperature a perfect mid-70s, with low humidity, and you are out for a walk. There's a spring in your step, a smile on your face, and everything seems perfect in your small sphere of influence. Why are you feeling so good in that scenario?

The answer: because everything is perfect; mind, body, and spirit are in tune. This can be your normal. Even if it were a cloudy sky, temps in the 50s, with a drizzle, your body, mind, and spirit, if they are in tune, would compensate. They would realign and your attitude would be of the former example. There would still be a purpose for your walk, purpose in your mind, and fulfillment of the spirit.

As we place food upon our tables and ask the Lord's blessing, we sit so far from the garden that because of the bastardization of what was once wholesome and nutritious we are unknowingly placed at risk. It is hard to know the truth and remain whole. Because of the GMOs (genetically modified organisms), the tainting of our food supply through the use of chemical preservatives, hormones, and over-processing to create shelf life, we are compromised. "What can I do?" you ask. Educate yourself, do the research, read labels. Whether they be *orgimicks* as I call them, or organic or not, follow the money, and it will tell you a lot on-line. Or for the brave ones, "drop-out" as we said in the 60s, and go find a piece of beautiful land and homestead, be radicalized even, and off-grid.

That's my goal, but I'm crazy. The important thing for each of us is to put it all in prayer and listen to the still, small voice.

Romans 14:7–8 reminds us, "For none of us liveth to himself, and no man dieth to himself. For whether we live, we live unto the Lord; and whether we die, we die unto the Lord: whether we live therefore, or die, we are the Lord's."

Physical Power Long Preserved: "Man came from the hand of his creator perfect in organization and beautiful in form. The fact that he has for six thousand years withstood the ever-increasing weight of disease and crime is conclusive proof of the power of endurance with which he was first endowed" (White, *Christian Temperance and Bible Hygiene*, p. 7).

You see, it is what we do, what we represent, in-between physical birth and the grave. It is how we choose to live our lives; but better still, it is for what reason, what purpose, and to whom you will dedicate your precious gift of yourself? And because of those choices, you will decide where you will spend eternity.

CHAPTER 5

Loving Thyself for Thy Neighbor's Sake

Every entity on earth, from the microscopic to the mighty leviathan, fights for survival and the continuation of their species. Man is the same but inherently different. We were granted a steward's dominion over all that is God's kingdom on earth. As we watch the ebb and flow of all life we cannot deny it is a miraculous ecosystem— everything has order, everything has purpose, and it is wonderfully made. Man is the determining factor whether it continues as it was naturally intended to be or whether it simply gets mucked up.

One cannot help another until they first help themselves; one cannot love another until they first love themselves just as God loves them. One of my late, dear mother's house rules was, "Before you and your brother move on to make another mess, clean up the one you're sitting in!" Basically stated, we must clean up the garbage in our own backyard before we move on to help our neighbor clean up the mess in their life. We must forgive ourselves by and through the mercy of Jesus Christ. Love one another is what Christ commanded His disciples to do and so we, as His modern-day disciples, must do the same. Watch, be aware, marvel, and witness the miracle of transformation that Jesus can accomplish in your life if only you allow Him to do so. Then take that which He has done for you and pay it forward to the world.

House cleaning of your holy temple, "your mind, body, and spirit," is a journey that begins with a first step, and the Holy Scriptures show us where to start concerning living a healthy lifestyle. Just because you live in your skin doesn't mean you own it. I know, I know … you don't like being told how you should live, how to dress, what you eat, drink, rub into your body, or what time you should go to bed, right? Sorry to tell you that this type of thinking is wrong on at least two counts: 1) God created man in His own image (Gen. 1:26, 27) and 2) Our gift of life maintains that we are stewards over our bodies and we are to glorify God with this temple. "What? know ye not that your body is the temple of the Holy Ghost which is in you, which ye have of God, and ye are not your own? For ye are bought with a price: therefore glorify God in your body, and in your spirit, which are God's" (1 Cor. 6:19, 20).

God has promised His people, in preparation for the holy kingdom, that "I will take sickness away from the midst of thee" (Exod. 23:25). God promised not to allow sickness to afflict His people provided they would keep all His commandments. So you ask, "What if I disregard the proper care of my body?" Remember in chapter 4 we talked about the man who was sitting beside the pool, fixed to a mat, waiting to get into the healing pool of water? This account is in John chapter 5, and Jesus considered the fact that this man had lived an unhealthy lifestyle which led up to his paralytic condition. Breaking a physical or moral law is considered a sin by our Creator. But also remember Jesus healed the man. John 5:14 tells us, "Afterward Jesus findeth him in the temple, and said unto him, 'Behold, thou art made whole: sin no more, lest a worse thing come unto thee.'" Ask yourself here and now, "Does this verse even remotely tell me that once you are saved, you are always saved?" No, it does not. "Go and sin no more" is what Christ tells us unless we want the same thing to happen again. Look also at John 8:11. It is the story about the adulteress and Christ tells her, "Neither do I condemn thee: go, and sin no more."

In preparation for God's holy kingdom we must remember that as we present our bodies to God we need to ask that He help us to cleanse our physical temple and make it into a holy sanctuary pleasing to Him.

In preparation for God's holy kingdom we must remember that as we present our bodies to God we need to ask that He help us to cleanse our physical temple and make it into a holy sanctuary pleasing to Him. "I beseech you therefore, brethren, by the mercies of God, that ye present your bodies a living sacrifice, holy, acceptable unto God, which is your reasonable service" (Rom. 12:1).

God in creation placed restrictions on diet. In the first chapter of Genesis we read, "And God said, behold I have given you every herb bearing seed, which is upon the face of all the earth, and every tree, in the which is the fruit of a tree yielding seed; to you it shall be for meat" (vs. 29). Deuteronomy 14:2, 3 tells us, "For thou art an holy people unto the LORD thy God, and the LORD hath chosen thee to be a peculiar people unto himself, above all the nations that are upon the earth. Thou shalt not eat any abominable thing."

So where does the Bible tell me what I should or should not eat? It is time to open the Bible once again and look over Leviticus chapter 11. The diet that was given us in the beginning did not include the flesh of animals. It was not until after the great flood when every green thing had been wiped off planet earth that man received permission to eat animal flesh. In choosing what man was to eat in Eden, God gave us the best diet; in the choice God made for us today He teaches us the same lesson. Through these choices we are trained so we might be a people for His own possession. Through us God desires us to go out and bless and teach the world.

In our past recorded in Bible history, as God brought the Israelites out of Egypt, He provided not flesh, but manna—"The Bread of

Heaven"—for them to eat. Complaints, grumbling, and murmurings of desire for the fleshpots of Egypt began and God recanted His original plan and the flesh of animals was included on the menu. But this was not to be forever. Just because it was allowed, doesn't mean that it was the ideal. The inclusion of animal products back then, and as it exists today, brings about death and disease to thousands. Because of the corruption of our animal's food supply today, it is passed forward, leaching into our world population.

Permission was granted for the eating of animal flesh but there are restrictions, and when you consider those restrictions, they make perfect sense and lessen unhealthy results. Swine flesh is definitely off the menu, as well as other animals, birds, and aquatic creatures. Eating of the fat and blood of accepted animals was also forbidden. Only animals that were in good condition could be used. The animal could not be torn up, or have died by itself, and the blood from which had to be properly drained. If all these conditions were not met, the use of that animal for food was prohibited. The explanation makes it sound gruesome, doesn't it? Imagine if you were the one doing the processing of an animal for food? (for further reading please see White, *Counsels on Diets and Foods*, p. 374).

By our departing from God's divine plan we have sown for ourselves a terrible loss. By continuing down this path we will not fulfill His purpose for us. The Lord will allow us to make such choices, but there is a sacrifice. Consider Psalm 106:13–15: "They soon forgat his works; they waited not for his counsel. But lusted exceedingly in the wilderness, and tempted God in the desert. And he gave them their request; but sent leanness into their soul." We need to be careful, cautious of what we wish for and what we pray for as it is not only God who is listening.

God's original intent and design for mankind was flawless. He never intended for any creature to fulfill another's culinary desire. There was to be no death in Eden, as the fruits of the garden were all man needed to complete his dietary requirements. Even before the flood man was eating animal flesh, much to God's displeasure, and it was because of man's worldly lusts that God said enough is enough. God out of necessity gave permission to Noah to eat of the clean animals that he had taken with him, knowing that it was not a healthy diet.

The three curses leading to our dilemma today are these: 1) The original sin of the disobedience of Adam and Eve engendered a posterity of lawlessness upon their descendants and the earth. 2) This curse through the shedding of blood fell upon the ground with the murder of Abel by Cain. 3) The most dreadful curse upon the earth was pronounced by God at the time of the flood.

"After the flood the people ate largely of animal food. God saw that the ways of man were corrupt, and that he was disposed to exalt himself proudly against his Creator and to follow the inclinations of his own heart. And He permitted that long-lived race to eat animal food to shorten their sinful lives. Soon after the flood the race began to rapidly decrease in size, and in length of years" (White, *Spiritual Gifts, vol. 4,* pp. 120, 121).

In all things I have done, including adopting a clean and proper diet, I attempted to include all matters concerning the human condition. Christ asks of us in our affairs respecting life on Earth that we give one hundred percent of our heart over to Him. By following Biblical guidelines concerning lifestyle changes I was simply told, "*Become more Christ-like.*" Coming from the world, it ain't easy! Admittedly, I am still a work in progress.

We must be careful as we swim about in a deep ocean full and teeming with ultra-distractions. As I who was once in a lucrative and responsible position found out, it is easy to be converted to a self-indulgent and extravagant lifestyle. Taking on such a lifestyle for my own sake I realized that no matter what was gained I could not afford it, but even if I was eventually able to, Christ-like principles do not allow for such foolishness. I realized that a myriad of Christ's teachings must be applied to alter my blind thinking. Let's think about the words found in Isaiah 28:9–13: "Whom shall he teach knowledge? and whom shall he make to understand doctrine? them that are weaned from the milk, and drawn from the breasts, For precept must be upon precept ... line upon line ... here a little, and there a little." The Word of God is to be patiently brought to the children and kept before them by parents who believe the Word of God. "For with stammering lips and another tongue will he speak to this people. To whom he said, This is the rest wherewith ye may cause the weary to rest; and this is the refreshing: yet they would not hear. But the word of the LORD was unto them precept upon precept; line upon line; here a little, and there a little; that they might go and fall backward, and be broken, and snared, and taken." WHY? Because they did not heed the Word of God which had been given them.

I could not simply choose my own wisdom over the instruction I had gathered from my Christian walk. I could not live life according to my own ideals. It is at the very least a most perplexing test—follow the Lord's counsel, or go my own way in how I think it should be. And the good Lord will graciously allow me to end up within a sure result of my own undoing; experience has personified this very fact. It happened when I chose a different direction, straying from the Lord's path. Advancing forward without prayer, without concern of what was in the Lord's best interest for me, for my family, was always a mistake.

In all our ways, in all our service to God, He speaks volumes to us if we would but listen and hear: "Give me thine heart" (Prov. 23:26).

It does not take much effort—God simply asks us to submit, to be a teachable, willing spirit. We who give to prayer its worthiness is the fact that it is breathed from a loving, obedient heart.

There are requirements to be of God's kingdom. Oh yes, there must be guidelines; and if you say, "I will not give you my heart to do this thing," that's okay; the Lord will allow you to move on in your supposed wise judgment without His heavenly wisdom until within you Isaiah 28:13 will be fulfilled.

We cannot say, "Okay, I will follow you Lord, but really ... you want me to give up what? But that takes me out of my comfort zone and it's not in harmony with my way of thinking. What will my family think and what about the opinions of my friends and colleagues?" Let the question always be asked before making any move, "Is this the will of the Lord?" Never let a major decision be based simply upon the opinions of others. Weigh all the facts before moving forward. Remember the world is full of opinions and everybody has one. Be a Biblical Berean and search for the truth in all matters. Acts 17:10–12 tells us who these Bereans were and why we should aspire to be like them today. "And the brethren immediately sent away Paul and Silas by night unto Berea: who coming thither went into the synagogue of the Jews. These were more noble than those in Thessalonica, in that they received the word with all readiness of mind, and searched the scriptures daily, whether those things were so. Therefore many of them believed; also of honourable women which were Greeks, and of men, not a few."

Acceptance, prayer, faith, love, and trust to be led by the Holy Spirit … I love Him who first loved me as yet a sinner. Christ died for me, took the stripes intended for me and my sins, and then died on a tree in my stead so that I may live.

Here we will stand in God's new kingdom. Isaiah 65:17, 18 promises: "For, behold, I create new heavens and a new earth: and the former shall not be remembered, nor come into mind. But be ye glad and rejoice for ever in that which I create: for, behold, I create Jerusalem a rejoicing, and her people a joy."

But you might ask, "What is God talking about here? I am not Jerusalem. I don't live there and I am not a Jew." Think of it this way: when the Jews rejected Christ as their Savior the commission was given to the gentiles. YOU are the new spiritual Jerusalem, we are the new spiritual Jerusalem, because we came, we saw, and we believed that Christ indeed died for us. Amen.

Let US within Christ's new spiritual body continue. Isaiah 65:19–25 expounds on the promises of joy and perfection to be found in heaven:

And I will rejoice in Jerusalem, and joy in my people: and the voice of weeping shall be no more heard in her, nor the voice of crying. There shall no more thence be an infant of days, nor an old man that hath not filled his days: for the child shall die an hundred years old; but the sinner being an hundred years old shall be accursed. And they shall build houses, and inhabit them; and they shall plant vineyards, and eat the fruit of them. They shall not build, and another inhabit; they shall not plant, and another eat: for as the days of a tree are the days of my people, and mine elect shall long enjoy the work of their hands. They shall not labour in vain, nor bring forth for trouble; for they are the seed of the blessed of the Lord, and their offspring with them. And it shall come to pass, that before they call, I will answer; and while they are yet speaking, I will hear. The wolf and the lamb shall feed together, and the lion shall eat straw like the bullock: and dust shall be the serpent's meat. They shall not hurt nor destroy in all my holy mountain, sayeth the LORD."

Allow God to work in you; let Him mold the clay. While yet as a human agent I devised and planned for myself something which God had withheld from me. It was rough for me as I complained and asked, "Why me, Lord? Why not me, Lord?" But as I placed my toe into the stirring spiritual water and submitted, placing into God's hands the clay that I am, God the Heavenly Potter began to mold, reshaping me into a vessel of honor. We as clay must submit, and if we let God as the Potter have His way, we can be worked and made into vessels as He sees fit for Christian service.

We as clay must submit, and if we let God as the Potter have His way, we can be worked and made into vessels as He sees fit for Christian service.

Let the hand of God work the clay as He knows just what kind of vessel He wants me to be. To every human He has given good work. God knows for what place you are fitted. We cannot work contrary to God, nor can we work contrary to each other in our service.

If self will submit to be worked, if you will cooperate with God, pray in unity, work in unity, all taking your place within the threads of life, then we can all be woven into a beautiful fabric that will glory and praise God's universal kingdom (Paraphrased from White, Letter 63, 1898).

Can a potter work without clay? Of course not! How could he? So, you see, if you do not provide God with the clay He cannot do the work in you. On a daily basis we must surrender to Him in order to overcome the trials we face and every day we will gain new victories. Our lives must be constantly cultivated, and this is how we will grow up into Christ. As God works the supple clay of our lives we will be fashioned according to His divine model (Paraphrased from White, Manuscript 55, 1900).

God will be justified before the entire universe. Isaiah 66: 22, 23 proclaims, "For as the new heavens and the new earth, which I will make, shall remain before me, saith the LORD, so shall your seed and your name remain. And it shall come to pass, that from one new moon to another, and from one sabbath to another, shall all flesh come to worship before me, saith the LORD."

Chapter 6

Our Historical Christian Legacy

The institution of the Sabbath was the second gift from God which Adam brought with him from out of the Garden of Eden. Remember in the last chapter we referred to two things that Adam would take with him when he and Eve were exiled from God's kingdom on earth? One was the divine institution of marriage and the other is the Sabbath rest.

"Thus the heavens and the earth were finished, and all the host of them. And on the seventh day God ended his work which he had made; and he rested on the seventh day from all his work which he made. And God blessed the seventh day, and sanctified it: because that in it he had rested from all his work which God created and made" (Gen. 2:1–3).

Genesis 2:2 and also Exodus 20:8–11 talk about a cycle of seven days. These are seven literal days, thus the weekly cycle of seven literal days is given with six for labor, and the seventh for rest. This Sabbath of rest has been preserved and brought down through Biblical history as a reminder of the great fact of the first seven days of our earth's history.

In Exodus 20:8–11 we find the fourth commandment given to Moses by God on Sinai:

Remember the sabbath day, to keep it holy. Six days shalt thou labour, and do all thy work. But the seventh day is the sabbath of the LORD thy God: in it thou shalt not do any work, thou, nor thy son, nor thy daughter, thy manservant, nor thy maidservant, nor thy cattle, nor thy stranger that is within thy gates. For in six days the LORD made heaven and earth, the sea, and all that in them is, and rested the seventh day: wherefore the LORD blessed the sabbath day, and hallowed it.

Sleep deprivation runs rampant throughout the United States and is the cause of many physical and mental disorders. Is it any wonder that in the Lord's kingdom He made provisions for a day of rest? Our God is not a God of confusion but the Author of order. "For God is not the author of confusion, but of peace, as in all churches of the saints" (1 Cor. 14:33).

I could list the entire *Decalogue* here, but I won't. This is the time for you who are reading this to get hold of a Bible, preferably the King James Version or the New King James Version, open it to Exodus 20, and read verses 1–17. You might be thinking, "The Ten Commandments—really? You want me to go down through them? I know them already." But do you—really? Pay special attention to verses 6, and then 8–11. Now notice there are TEN Commandments … not eight … not nine … but TEN. Aside from verse 6 which tells that if we love the Lord we should keep these commandments, there is another commandment of importance which Jesus added in the New Testament when asked by an attorney of his day in a feeble attempt to trip Him up in matters of the law. Matthew 22:36–40 tells the story: "Master, which is the greatest commandment in the law? Jesus said unto him, Thou shalt love the Lord thy God with all thy heart, and with all thy soul, and with all thy mind. This is the first and great commandment. And the second is like unto it, Thou shalt love thy neighbor as thyself. On these two commandments hang all the law and the prophets." Remember the title of the last Chapter? "Love Thyself for Thy Neighbor's Sake."

If you go through training to become an investigator for the US Department of the Treasury or the FBI, you will one day find yourself learning what funny money looks and feels like and how to tell the difference between it and the real thing. Before a bogus note is ever placed before you there will be exhaustive study about the real deal so that when you have placed in your hand a counterfeit you will immediately know the difference. And so it goes with our Christian journey.

No one likes to be lied to. No one likes to be robbed. And life is no joke—not one millisecond of our future existence and happiness is guaranteed, so don't mess with my comfort zone, right? Don't keep me in the dark—tell me the truth … I can take it. Seriously, though, along with the birth of the Child of Truth came accountability for all who would recognize Him. Whoa, did you say *accountability*? That's a heavy burden, man, and I am not sure I want to go down that road.

I was twelve years old or so and it was breakfast time and my grandma had just served me a bowl of oat-groats and a plate of French toast. She sat down beside me and put some maple syrup on her French toast and as she passed the syrup to me, she gave me a concerned look and said, "Remember someday what I'm about to tell you. Know that we don't worship on the correct day and the Catholic System is the beast that's talked about in the Bible."

My question to Grandma was, "What are you talking about? We go to church every Sunday like you and Mom have taught us."

"That's what tradition has brought to us; it's not what the Scriptures tell us to do," Grandma stated.

I was a little upset, even at twelve years old, thinking I had been duped, and stated, "I just got baptized, Grandma. I studied to do that, and nowhere did it tell me that Sunday was wrong."

"You were baptized into the body of Christ Jesus, not to any particular man-made curriculum or tradition. In that I have comfort and certainty. You are now part and parcel to Jesus Christ. He now owns you and the Holy Spirit will guide and protect you," Grandma said assuring me that I was not in error for my decision and added, "Go easy on the maple syrup."

"I hope that I did the right thing Grandma," I told her, but is was more of a question.

"You are now a small candle, a light that will one day help to light the world," she said with a smile.

I remembered that incident about ten years ago when I was trying to discredit what light my wife had been given concerning the correct Sabbath day of worship and which she was desperately trying to convey to me. As you can see, the light bulb did come on, and I am now a Sabbath keeper.

But what was Grandma saying about tradition and man-made curriculum? Everything that I will touch upon is based on the principles and teachings of Jesus Christ. Understand that I bear no malice or evil thought towards anyone on this planet, living or dead. It is as my Master and Savior Jesus said, "I have sheep in many pastures". We read this in John 10:16— "And other sheep I have, which are not of this fold: them also I must bring, and they shall hear my voice; and there shall be one fold, and one shepherd."

There are good Christians in all denominations. It is the Catholic order and traditional system of things to which I take issue. I blame all this on my dear grandmother. Bessie was her name, and what she said to her then twelve-year-old grandson lit a spark, planted a seed, which at that time I was clueless about. Note that she and her ancestry were from the Austrian/Switzerland area and she was very well versed in the Bible (she had a "High German Bible" which in fact was a Martin Luther version published in the 1700s and is now in my possession). Placing the Good News of Jesus Christ into the common man's hands is what Martin Luther made possible. This is what he was condemned for wanting to do. Grandma was also very aware about the history of the Reformation. "This is why we came to America," she would say, "to escape oppression and persecution."

This was a prophecy fulfilled. (Open your Bible to Revelation 13:11–12 and take a read.) My grandmother said, "Larry, remember these two things." 1) We do not worship on the correct day. 2) The Catholic traditional system is the beast.

We will discuss the Reformation and what scripture tells us about it and why it is important to finish what was started so long ago. Those words that were so carefully, divinely inspired by God to be written down by the prophets, is about what holds us in a continual battle of controversy today. It started with the degradation of the Lord's truth by the Romanist system. The Reformists fought through that time of spiritual darkness and spiritual slavery that went along with it. They gave their time and their lives for this mission. They were hunted down to be silenced, but they prevailed. Proof of their victory is that we sit here today, free to worship God as we will. They were the small voices crying out in the wilderness: "The voice of him that crieth in the wilderness, Prepare ye the way of the LORD, make straight in the desert a highway for our God" (Isa. 40:3).

We need the Living Water here and now; we need the seeds of truth and the kingdom life planted around us in order for love, understanding, and salvation to take hold in the rocky ground and bear fruit.

I look at our world at times and see that starving desert of humanity, bereft of understanding, void of love, where no good can flower and grow. We need the Living Water here and now; we need the seeds of truth and the kingdom life planted around us in order for love, understanding, and salvation to take hold in the rocky ground and bear fruit. That Water, Truth, and Life is none other than our Lord and Savior Jesus Christ.

The world is going to hate us. Jesus told us that in John 15:18–25. Please go to your Bible and take a read as I do not want you to think I am making any of this up!

Again, the world hates the truth found in Christ's words; they find them inconvenient. Jesus' message of peace, love, and salvation for all mankind —people of the world find no purchase in it, because in their hearts there is no understanding or need of such things.

I will here quote from Ellen G. White's *The Great Controversy* (p. 189– 191) a historical vignette from the life of Martin Luther. It is concerning his return to clarify the morphing of the understanding of the Luther doctrine based upon the understanding of Jesus Christ. At one point Luther had taken a hiatus from the grueling task he had undertaken only to have a shroud of mystery and violence overtake him within an evil cloak of corrupt teachings. With great caution and humility, and yet with decision and firmness, he entered upon his work.

"By the word," said he, "must we overthrow and destroy what has been set up by violence. I will not make use of force against the superstitious unbelieving ... No one must be constrained. Liberty is the very essence of faith."

It was soon noised through Wittenberg that Luther had returned and that he was to preach. The people flocked from all directions, and the church was filled to overflowing. Ascending the pulpit, he with great wisdom and gentleness instructed, exhorted, and reproved. Touching the course of some who had resorted to violent measures in abolishing the mass, he said:

"The mass is a bad thing. God is opposed to it; it ought to be abolished; and I would that throughout the whole world it were replaced by the supper of the gospel. But let no one be torn from it by force. We must leave the matter in God's hands. His word must act and not we. And why so, you will ask? Because I do not hold men's hearts in my hand, as the potter holds the clay. We have the right to speak: we have not the right to act. Let us preach; the rest belongs to God. Were I to employ force, what should I gain? Grimace, formality, apings, human ordinances, and hypocrisy ... But there would be no sincerity of heart, nor faith, nor charity. Where these three are wanting, all is wanting, and I would not give a pear stalk for such a result. ... God does more by His word alone than you and I and all the world by our united strength. God lays hold upon the heart; and when the heart is taken, all is won.

I will preach, discuss, and write; but I will constrain none, for faith is a voluntary act. See what I have done. I stood up against the pope, indulgences, and papists, but without violence or tumult. I put forward God's word; I preached and wrote – this was all I did. And yet while I was asleep, ... the word that I had preached overthrew popery, so that neither prince or emperor has done it so much harm, and yet I did nothing; the word alone did it all. If I had wished to appeal force, the whole of Germany would perhaps been deluged with blood. But what would have been the result? Ruin, desolation both to body and soul. I therefore kept quiet, and left the Word to run through the world alone."

The Word of God broke the spell of fanatical excitement. The power of the gospel alone brought back the misguided people into the way of truth.

Matthew 5:11 tells us, "Blessed are ye, when men shall revile you, and persecute you, and shall say all manner of evil against you falsely, for my sake." And it is also written in Matthew 5:44, "But I say unto you, Love your enemies, bless them that curse you, do good to them that hate you, and pray for them that despitefully use you, and persecute you."

John Wycliffe was another considered a heretic by the Romanists during the 13th century in England. Wycliffe used Genesis 15:1 to give him strength and it reads, "Fear not ... I am thy shield and thy exceeding great reward." Wycliffe, like his Master Jesus, was not content to preach the gospel to just the poor, spreading the light in their humble homes in his own parish in Lutterworth, England. No, he wanted it carried to every part of England, rich or poor, freeman, slave, and nobleman. As a professor of theology at Oxford he preached in the halls of the university. So faithful was he that they named him "the gospel doctor." But the greatest work of his life would be the translation of the Scriptures into the English language so that it could be accessible to all. He stated, "I want this translation to be, so that every man in England might read, in the language in which he was born, the wonderful works of God" (White, *The Great Controversy*, p. 87).

Suddenly Wycliffe was taken ill, and the vultures began to circle. He was only sixty years of age. But the unceasing toil and the impending encroachment of his enemies ever lurking about, took their toll. Hearing that Wycliffe was bedridden by a dangerous illness the Romanists were poised, ready to strike. Now, the enemy thought, *he will surely, bitterly repent the evil he has done to the church*, and they hurried to his bed chamber to bear witness to Wycliffe's last and final confession. Representatives from the four orders, with four civil officers, gathered about the dying man's bed. "You have death on your lips," they said, "be touched by your faults, retract in our presence all that you have said to our injury."

The Reformer listened in silence to their request; then he asked his attendant to raise him up on the bed. Gazing steadily upon them with a wary eye, as they stood waiting for his recantation, Wycliffe mustered his God-given energy and said boldly in the firm, strong voice which had so often caused them to tremble: "I shall not die, but live; and declare the evil deeds of the friars!" Upon hearing those words the monks scurried like rats from a burning ship.

Wycliffe lived and his words were fulfilled. He placed into his countrymen's hands the most powerful of all weapons against Rome— The Holy Bible, the Heaven-appointed agent to liberate, enlighten, and evangelize the people. Through the translation of the Bible he did more to break the chains of ignorance and vice, more to liberate and elevate his country, than was ever achieved by the most brilliant victories on the field of battle. Wycliffe had placed into English hands a light which should never be extinguished. "In Him was life; and the life was the light of men. And the light shineth in the darkness; and the darkness comprehended it not" (John 1:4, 5).

Matthew 5:16 says for us to, "Let your light so shine before men, that they may see your good works, and glorify your Father which is in heaven." Jesus Christ died for our liberty—Amen. Liberty of life … our freedom to choose. The freedom of choice could not happen without firsthand knowledge and personal understanding of what it is that sets men's souls free. That is what the Reformation was all about. It was the taking away of the power of the Romanists to dictate and interpret to their own advantage the apostolic message, turning it from love of life into a life of apostasy. But how could this have happened?

The Chain That Leads Us to Present Day Truth …

Rome made claim to their position of power through the bastardization of scripture:

Matthew 16:18, 19: "And I say also unto thee, That thou art Peter, and upon this rock I will build my church; and the gates of hell shall not prevail against it. And I will give unto thee the keys of the kingdom of heaven: and whatsoever thou shalt bind on earth shall be bound in heaven: and whatsoever thou shalt loose on earth thou shall be loosed in heaven."

Luke 22:32: "But I have prayed for thee, that thy faith fail not: and when thou art converted, strengthen thy brethren."

John 21:15–17: "So when they had dined, Jesus saith unto Simon Peter, Simon, son of Jonas, lovest thou me more than these? He saith unto him, Yea, Lord, thou knowest that I love thee. He saith unto him, Feed my lambs. He saith to him again the second time, Simon, son of Jonas, lovest thou me? He saith unto him, Yea Lord; thou knowest that I love thee. He saith unto him, Feed my sheep. He saith unto him the third time, Simon, son of Jonas, lovest thou me? And he said unto him, Lord, thou knowest all things; thou knowest that I love thee. Jesus saith unto him, Feed my sheep."

Both St. Paul and St. Peter were martyred in Rome. Clearly they believed that these verses told the popes that they were the custodians of the Christian Church, including the keys to heaven. Some of the power of the papacy was based on Biblical passages, but some is derived on political cultural realities. The following discussion of the history of Rome and Protestantism is based on the chapter, "Liberty of Conscience," in *The Great Controversy* by Ellen White (pp. 564–582).

Investiture Struggle endured between the Emperor and the Pope until Constantine, in March of AD 313, gave a separate and all-inclusive seat to the pope. In 606 Emperor Phocas, a murderous, adulterer, gave Pope Boniface III the declaration that the Bishop of Rome was pre-eminent— spiritually supreme—and from that time forward the popes held their authority neither from the emperor nor from Rome but from Heaven.

Blasphemy? The Bishop of Rome claimed not to be the Chief Bishop and the first of Patriarchs, but the Vicar of the Most-High God, not to be contested. What an echo of Isaiah 14:13–15: "For thou hast said in thine heart, I will ascend into heaven, I will exalt my throne above the stars of God: I will sit also upon the mount of congregation, in the sides of the north. I will ascend above the heights of the clouds; I will be like the most High. Yet thou shalt be brought down to hell, to the sides of the pit." Again, we find another link.

Going Back to Basic Bible Principles—AD 1179 to 1218 Peter Waldo (Valdes) was called by a local name, "The Waldensians," which became "The Poor in Christ," "The Poor in Spirit," and "Brothers" (presenting basic Bible teaching to the masses).

Obedience—The Morovian Church—AD 1369 to 1415. John Huss was burned at the stake for heresy against the doctrines of the Catholic Church on July 6, 1415. These "heresies" included the debate of ecclesiology, the Eucharist, or claiming obedience to the Holy Communion as Christ intended. He stated that the Papal Office was not given by divine command, that the communion observance was in its entirety for all true believers and not exclusive to the Papal order. Certain people were only allowed to partake of the body of Christ, not receiving the Holy Sacrament of wine.

Grace—The Lutheran Church—Martin Luther. November 10, 1483 to February 18, 1546. Martin Luther first printed the Bible into German. He led the 16th century Reformation revolt in Germany against the Papacy.

After posting his Ninety-five Theses (questions on indulgences and justification by faith) he was asked if he believed that the death of Jan Hus was unjust. He said that he believed that it was, and thus his answer brought about the question of the whole authority of the Pope and the Papal Council.

Growth—Calvinists, Huguenot Missionaries—John Calvin. July 10, 1509 to May 27, 1564. From Geneva, Switzerland, they spread across Europe their message of truth based strictly upon scriptures. They used Psalms instead of songs sung in the church, totally modeled after apostolic times with a strict division of church and state.

Baptism by Immersion—The Anabaptists (Mennonites)— Menno Simmons. Sometime in 1496 to January 31, 1561. Menno Simmons preached the rejection of infant baptism and left the priesthood to follow Christ. Menno believed in asceticism after conversion to the point of how one views and deals with the "Worldly Society" afterward. The "Bride of Christ" he considered to be the church as a whole waiting for Christ's return.

Holiness—The Methodist Church—John Wesley. June 28, 1704 to March 2, 1791. Founder of the Holiness Movement and believer in the reformed doctrine of justification of faith, Wesley found his calling in open air and lay preaching to the neglected, poor, and most needy— those who were rejected and would not go into an organized church body. His revival- style preaching brought him great recognition, and even those in the Morovian church looked down on him as peculiar. He organized his church by the viewpoint of Apostolic Succession.

Martyrs: Hugh Latimer and Nicholas Ridley. Burned at the stake on October 16, 1555 for heresy against Catholic doctrine. Latimer said to

Ridley as they were about to be burned, "Be of good cheer Master Ridley, and play the man; for we shall this day light such a candle in England as I trust by God's grace shall never be put out."

Martyr: Thomas Cranmer. Burned at the stake in Oxford, England on March 21 for heresy against Catholic doctrine. Born July 2, 1489 and died March 21, 1556, he was the architect of the Anglican *Book of Common Prayer*. Cranmer was an English leader of the Reformation. He was dubbed Arch Bishop of Canterbury and was advisor to King Henry VIII.

Sabbath—The Re-establishment of All Ten Commandments— William Miller, founder of the Millerite Movement. 1833. This led to the establishment of the Seventh-day Adventist Church as we know it today. Isaiah 58:13 and 14 tells us, "If thou turn away thy foot from the sabbath, from doing thy pleasure on my holy day; and call the sabbath a delight, the holy of the LORD, honourable; and shalt honour him, not doing thine own ways, nor finding thine own pleasure, nor speaking thine own words: Then shalt thou delight thyself in the LORD; and I will cause thee to ride upon the high places of the earth, and feed thee with the heritage of Jacob thy father: for the mouth of the LORD hath spoken it."

Many other verses address God's desire for us to keep all of His commandments.

John 14:15: "If ye love me, keep my commandments."

John 15:10–11: "If ye keep my commandments, ye shall abide in my love; even as I have kept my Father's commandments, and abide in his love. These things have I spoken unto you, that my joy might remain in you, and that your joy might be full."

1 John 2:4: "He that saith, I know him, and keepeth not his commandments, is a liar, and the truth is not in him."

Romans 2:13: "For not the hearers of the law are just before God, but the doers if the law shall be justified."

Romans 3:31: "Do we then make void the law through faith? God forbid: yea, we establish the law."

2017 marked another great pivotal point in earth's history for Christianity. Five hundred years ago Martin Luther nailed his Ninety-Five Thesis onto the cathedral door in Wittenberg, calling out the improprieties of the Catholic system. Last year many factions of the Protestant churches around the world wrote a letter of apology to Pope Francis stating that they had been wrong by moving away from the "Mother Church" and calling out their desire to return and align themselves once again within the Romanist order.

Now Pope Francis is indeed one of the most affable Popes ever to exist. His agenda to bring together all peoples to align in what he calls a "coming together" of world leaders for the benefit of all mankind is ambitious and worthy of note. The other fact is that he is calling for accountability of injustices both past and present. Hence the Pope apologized to the world. Realizing that the Church of Rome had made grievous errors in the past, now they want to make amends and heal the wound of social radicalism. Apology accepted? If so, can a leopard so easily change its spots?

Realizing that the Church of Rome had made grievous errors in the past, now they want to make amends and heal the wound of social radicalism.

Question: Have these persons forgotten the claims of infallibility put forth for over 800 years by this haughty world power? So far from being relinquished, this claim was affirmed in the nineteenth century with greater positivity than ever before. As Rome asserts that the "church never erred; nor will it, according to the scriptures, ever err" (Mosheim, *Institutes of Ecclesiastical History, Ancient and Modern,* book 3, century 11, part 2, ch. 2, sec. 9, note 17). How can she, "The Mother Church," renounce the principles which governed her course in past ages?

"The papal church will never relinquish her claim to infallibility for it has not shown any humility in the past. Consider all that she has done in her persecution of those who reject her dogmas she holds to be right; and would she not repeat the same acts, should the opportunity be presented? Let the restraints now imposed by the secular governments be removed and Rome be reinstated to her former power" (White, *The Great Controversy,* p. 564). (NEWS FLASH: on February 11, 1929, the "Papal Wound" was healed in a document known as the Lateran Concordat. This historic document was signed by Benito Mussolini, representing the Italian government, and Cardinal Gasparri for Pope

Pius XI and the Vatican, thus re-establishing the political power and diplomatic standing of the Roman Catholic Church. This had been lost when Italy seized Rome, the last of the Papal States, on September 20th, 1870). Following this there would speedily be "a revival of her tyranny and persecution" (ibid.). (Note: this was after World War I, but right before Adolf Hitler and Benito Mussolini became major political leaders).

There are many who are disposed to attribute any fear of Roman Catholicism in the United States to bigotry or childishness. Such see nothing in the character and attitude of Romanism that is hostile to our free institutions, or find nothing portentous in its growth. Let us then, first compare some of the fundamental principles of our government with those of the Catholic Church.

The Constitution of the United States guarantees liberty of conscience. Nothing is dearer or more fundamental. Pope Pius IX, in his Encyclical Letter of August 15, 1854, said: "The absurd and erroneous doctrines or ravings in defense of liberty of conscience are a most pestilential err – a pest, of all others, most to be dreaded in a state." The same pope, in his Encyclical Letter of December 8, 1864, anathematized "those who assert the liberty of conscience and of religious worship," also "all such as maintain that the church may not employ force."

The pacific tone of Rome in the United States does not imply a change of heart. She is tolerant where she is helpless. (White, The Great *Controversy*, pp. 564–65)

Daniel 8:24, 25 tells us, "And his power shall be mighty, but not by his own power: and he shall destroy wonderfully, and shall prosper, and practise, and shall destroy the mighty and the holy people. And through his policy also he shall cause craft to prosper in his hand; and he shall magnify himself in his heart, and by peace shall destroy many: he shall also stand up against the Prince of princes; but he shall be broken without hand."

Says Bishop O'Connor: "Religious liberty is endured until the opposite can be carried into effect without peril to the Catholic world." The Archbishop of St. Louis once said: "Heresy and unbelief are crimes; and in Christian countries, as in Italy and Spain for instance, where all people are Catholics, and where the Catholic religion is an essential part of the law of the land they are punished as other crimes." (White, *The Great Controversy*, p. 565)

NOTE: "Every Cardinal, Archbishop, and Bishop in the Catholic Church takes an oath of allegiance to the pope, in which occur the following words: 'Heretics, schismatics, and rebels to our said lord (the pope), or his aforesaid successors, I will to my utmost persecute and oppose'" (Strong, *Our Country*, Ch. 5, para. 2–4).

It is true there are true Christians in the Roman Catholic communion. Thousands serving in that church are serving God according to the best light they have. The Catholic Church still reserves the right to interpret the Bible in the light of her own tradition, thus justifying those doctrines that do not harmonize with biblical teachings (White, *The Great Controversy*, Appendix, explanation of p. 340).

Romanism as a system is no more in harmony with the gospel of Christ now than at any formal period in her history. The Protestant churches are in great darkness, or they would discern the signs of the times. The Roman church is far reaching in her plans and modes of operation. She is employing every device to extend her influence and increase her power in preparation for a fierce and determined conflict to gain control of the world, to establish persecution, and undo all that Protestantism has done. Catholicism is gaining ground on every side of the world today. Protestants have tampered with and patronized popery; they have made compromises and concessions which papist themselves are surprised to see and fail to understand. (White, *The Great Controversy*, pp. 565–566)

A joint declaration by the Catholic Church Pontifical Council for promoting Christian Unity and the Lutheran World Federation occurred on October 31, 1999, concerning the doctrine of justification. As a result of extensive ecumenical dialogue, it states that the churches now share "a common understanding of our justification by God's grace through faith in Christ; that is to the parties involved in this signing this document resolves the 500-year-old conflict over the nature of justification which was at the root of the Protestant Reformation" (Wikipedia, http://1ref.us/ri, accessed 1/21/19). The World Methodist Council also adopted the declaration on July 18, 2006. And to top it off, as was referred to earlier in this book, last year on October 31, 2017, The World Communion of Reformed Churches (representing the "80 million members of Congregational Presbyterian, Reformed, United, Uniting, and Waldensian churches") adopted the declaration.

Note: not all Catholics or Christian factions and synods go along with or share the views of those signing these declarations.

In substance, the Pontifical Council on Promotion of Christian Unity (PCPCU) and the Lutheran World Federation acknowledge in declaration that the excommunications relating to the doctrine of justification set forth by the Council of Trent do not apply to the teachings of the Lutheran churches set forth in the text; likewise, the churches acknowledged that the condemnations set forth in the Lutheran Confessions do not apply to the Catholic teachings on justification set forth in the document.

> Support for the joint declaration was not universal among Lutherans. Of the 124 members of the Lutheran World Federation, thirty-five cast votes against the JDDJ [Joint Declaration on Doctrine of Justification]; these included many churches who are also members of the International Lutheran Church. Member churches of the Confessional Evangelical Lutheran Conference even stated that "JDDJ ... should be repudiated by all Lutherans."

Some Catholics have raised other objections. [They] contend that the Lutheran signers do not have the required authority to represent their communities ([because], from a Catholic perspective, they are not full churches) and, therefore, that no Lutheran can make the agreement binding on the constituents of the Lutheran World Federation. (Wikipedia, http://1ref.us/ri, accessed 1/21/19).

After all the pomp and circumstance fades, after all the smoke clears from the sacrificial fires, and the agony and suffering of the martyrs subsides, what has been accomplished?

Pastor C.A. Murry, in his sermon series "Daniel All Access" aired on 3ABN (January 29, 2019), shared that during the year 1551 at the meeting of the Council of Trent in northern Italy, Arch Bishop Reggio addressed the problem of Protestant inconsistency in the area of *Solo Scriptura* in this statement:

The written word explicitly enjoins the observance of the seventh day as the Sabbath. We (Catholics) do not observe the seventh day. If they (Protestants) do truly hold the scripture alone as their standard they would be observing the 7th day as is enjoined in the scripture (The Bible) throughout. Yet they (Protestants) not only reject the observance of the Sabbath enjoined in the written word (The Bible) but they have adopted and do practice the observance of Sunday for which they have only the tradition of the church (Mother Church/Catholic System).

Consequently the claim of scripture alone (Bible alone ie: *Solo Scriptura)* as their standard fails and the doctrine of scripture and tradition as essential (Catholic doctrine of Sunday as being the Lord's day of worship) is fully established. The Protestants themselves being (their own) judges. Spring 1551.

Twenty years later, at a meeting called the Augsburg Confession, Arch Bishop Reggio again spoke out concerning Protestant inconsistencies in the Protestant Reformation, calling it an "unwarranted revolt" against the Catholic Church.

The argument as stated is a powerful one. What the Archbishop is stating here, in my opinion, is that the Protestants themselves do not believe what they are teaching in the doctrine of "The Bible and the Bible alone."

Wow, I think I feel my own toes are being stepped on. I have to ask myself, "Am I walking the path of Jesus? Am I following Solo Scriptura?"

When the question of Protestant inconsistency was placed before Malachi Martin, his comment was as follows: "If you worship the Lord on the day designated by the Catholic Church regardless what you call yourself, you are Catholic."

So it doesn't matter what we call ourselves—Lutheran, Presbyterian, Methodist, Church of Christ—if you worship on Sunday, the day given for traditional worship by the Catholic system, that makes you Catholic.

The gulf between how fully I can love and how fully God wishes that I love my fellow human beings is vast.

Putting all the politics aside, it boils down to be a personal issue and understanding—how do I recover from the damage done by my Eden parents? How do I recover from that original sin? The gulf between how fully I can love and how fully God wishes that I love my fellow human beings is vast. How can I recover from the damage and how am I saved and made right in God's heavenly kingdom eyes? Stated succinctly in reformation terms—justified. Do I crawl my way out, fighting tooth and nail, or is it a gift called amnesty?

Our deepest struggle has been around the doctrine of the gift of grace. The New Testament gives us various discussions of the term. Paul writes in Romans 1:17 about righteous by faith and mentions it again in Ephesians 2:4–10: "For by grace you have been saved through faith" (NKJV). Apostle James writes in James 2:17 "faith, if it hath not works, is dead." Apostle Paul seems to strike a balance in Galatians 5:6: "but faith which worketh by love."

It is not complicated and to put it in modern terms: "It ain't rocket science."

When Europe emerged from the Dark Ages the main question was, "Is grace a gift, and if not how do I earn it?" This was the abyss between the Catholics and the Reformists. At that time there were many excesses in Catholic practice, and it was felt that they could earn salvation in a myriad of ways. Luther being a perfectionist in his own right was probably driven mad over the pressure of having to do so many things to remain in God's grace. We see here a parallel between this situation and the yoke which the Jewish governing body placed upon their people to remain faithful. Jesus saw their error and called them out for it. And look what happened to Him…

Luther came to understand through scripture, specifically the writings of the apostle Paul, that God's grace is freely given. Luther saw, and eventually so did many, that the Catholic system was in deep need of reform. For evidence let's look back at an example from our Christian family tree in the form of a letter requesting an answer (http://1ref.us/rj, accessed 12/23/2018):

From: J. L. Day Thomaston, Georgia Date: May 22, 1954

To: Pope Pius XII

Dear Sir,

Is the accusation true, that Protestants accuse you of? They say you changed the seventh day Sabbath to the, so called, Christian Sunday: Identical with the first day of the week. If so, when did you make the change, and by what authority?

Yours truly,

J. L. Day

The Reply:

THE CATHOLIC EXTENSION MAGAZINE

180 Wabash Ave, Chicago, Illinois

(Under the Blessing of Pope Pius XI)

Dear Sir:

Regarding the change from the observance of the Jewish Sabbath to the Christian Sunday, I wish to draw your attention to the facts:

(That Protestants, who accept the Bible as the only rule of faith and 1 religion, should by all means go back to the observance of the Sabbath.

) The fact that they do not, but on the contrary observe Sunday, stultifies them in the eyes of every thinking man.

(We Catholics do not accept the Bible as the only rule of faith. Besides 2 the Bible we have the living church, the authority of the church, as rule

) to guide us. We say, this church instituted by Christ, to teach and guide men through life, has the right to change the ceremonial laws of the Old Testament and hence, we accept her change of the Sabbath to Sunday. We frankly say, "yes, the Church made this change, made this law, as she made many other laws, for instance, the Friday Abstinence, the unmarried priest-Catholic marriages, and a thousand other laws.

(We also say that of all the Protestants, the Seventh-day Adventist[s] are 3 the only group that reason correctly and are consistent with their

) teachings. It is always somewhat laughable to see the Protestant Churches, in pulpit and legislature, demand the observance of Sundays of which there is nothing in the Bible.

With best wishes,

Peter R. Tramer, Editor

So as we make an assessment looking within ourselves we see that, yes, I too am in need of a reformation. Let's continue our investigation into who we are and what we are about.

CHAPTER 7

Fellowship Is Where Faith Blossoms

Faith is works by and through our outpouring of love. How do I do that and where is there an example of this in the Bible? The book of Acts, brothers and sisters, is a prime example. Let's open up the Manual to Basic Instruction—Before Leaving Planet Earth, or in other words, the Bible. Fellowship began here in Acts and continues until this very day.

Acts 2:42–47 is about the devotion and increase of the infant church ... say, could that be you?

And they continued steadfastly in the apostles' doctrine and fellowship, and in breaking of bread, and in prayers. And fear came upon every soul: and many wonders and signs were done by the apostles. And all that believed were together, and had all things in common; And sold their possessions and goods, and parted them to all men, as every man had need. And they, continuing daily with one accord in the temple, and breaking bread from house to house, did eat their meat with gladness and singleness of heart. Praising God, and having favour with all the people. And the Lord added to the church daily such as should be saved.

God can breathe new life into every soul that sincerely desires to serve Him, and can touch the lips with the efficiency of fire. The Lord will provide you with the words, and He will give you eloquence of His praises. He will give you the gift of voice and you will be imbued with the power to speak forth the wonderful truths of God's Word. If you have a stammering tongue it will be unfurled; in your timidity you will find strength and bear courageous testimony for truth. This he did not just for Peter the gregarious one, but for all the apostles, and since you are now learning to become His apostle, He will do the same for you.

After you have accepted Christ and are baptized into the faith, people will begin to marvel at your transformation. As you commune with your new brothers and sisters you will find fellowship and spiritual sustenance as you move forward on the pathway to God's kingdom.

We should not inquire or wonder about what is the practice of men, or what is the custom of the world, when matters of our individual walk with Jesus are concerned. Do not ask, "How shall I behave or act in order to have the approval of men?" or "What will the world tolerate?" The question of intense interest to every newbie in the walk of faith should be, "What does God say?" In order to find out we must daily read His Sacred Book, and obey it, not wavering on any word and adhering to His requirements. 2 Corinthians 6:17–18 tells us, "Wherefore come out from among them, and be ye separate, saith the Lord, and touch not the unclean thing; and I will receive you. And will be a Father unto you, and ye shall be my sons and daughters, saith the Lord Almighty."

Acts 4:32–34 tells us more about the early church. "And the multitude of them that believed were of one heart and of one soul; neither said any of them that ought of the things which he possessed was his own; but they had all things in common. And with great power gave the apostles witness of the resurrection of the Lord Jesus: and great grace was upon them all. Neither was there any among them that lacked: for as many as were possessors of lands or houses sold them, and brought the prices of the things that were sold."

We are not saying here to go out and sell all your worth as there is nothing wrong with possessions, but it is about the intent. "Render to Caesar the things that are Caesar's, and to God the things that are

God's" (Mark 12:17) and pay forward (share) to those in need what God's goodness has given to you.

Isaiah 58:7: "Is it not to deal thy bread to the hungry, and that thou bring the poor that are cast out to thy house? when thou seest the naked, that thou cover him; and that thou hide not thyself from thine own flesh?"

Hebrews 10:23–25: "Let us hold fast the profession of our faith without wavering; (for he is faithful that promised;) And let us consider one another to provoke unto love and to good works; Not forsaking the assembling of ourselves together, as the manner of some is; but exhorting one another: and so much the more, as ye see the day approaching."

Do not let your thoughts dwell continually upon self. Think of Jesus. He is not in His holy place locked down in solitude and grandeur, but He is surrounded by the angels waiting to do their Master's bidding. And yes, if that be you calling out for help, Jesus will send them straight away to work for the weakest saint who puts his trust in God. All— whether high or low, rich or poor—have access and the same help will be provided. Cell phones, emails, texts are not needed—just prayerful perseverance.

John 1:14: "The Word became flesh and made His dwelling among us" (NIV).

In your mind and in my mind are ideas, thoughts that are abstract, until we give them life in the form of voice or writ. Once conveyed they take form and shape concept. That is what Christ did when He came into the world to tell us what God was like, both by His words and deeds. Now man could begin to understand because the Word became flesh. Christ came here with a specific mission in mind.

John 3:17: "For God did not send his Son into the world to condemn the world, but to save the world through him" (NIV). Included in Jesus' last prayer before His death are the words, "As you sent me into the world, I have sent them into the world" (John 17:18, NIV). Jesus is talking here about all His followers, and that includes not just the apostles of olden days but, yes, you guessed it right—you and me and all sisters and brothers expressing the faith of our Lord and Savior.

There is a role to play and it is not any different from what Matthew, Mark, Luke, John, Paul, and Jesus Himself played.

We must ensure that the Word becomes flesh and we do it the same way Jesus did—by clarity of thought, action and deed, by and through the way we live (lead by example). The reference you provide is a starting point from where others will derive their understanding of what and who God is. What? Yes, we the lowly will attempt to place the world upon our shoulders and become accountable not only for our own actions, but to instill in the minds of our children, spouses, parents, aunts, uncles, neighbors, and friends, and those we meet and greet on a day-to-day basis, the love and understanding of Jesus Christ.

There is no difference between witnessing and fellowship. This may seem strange, but fellowship is the witness. Let's look at John 13:35: "By this everyone will know that you are my disciples, **if you love one another**" (NIV, emphasis added). That is the litmus test, isn't it? You mean I have to love my boss? You mean I have to love that crazy woman who works at my job and goes out of her way to put me down? You mean I have to care about that dirty old man who is always throwing inappropriate innuendos at me?

It may be unpleasant, but that is the irrefutable argument. We learn in 1 John 4:20–21, "If a man say, I love God; and hateth his brother, he is a liar: for he that loveth not his brother who he hath seen, how can he love God whom he hath not seen? And this commandment have we from him, That he who loveth God loveth his brother also."

Let's also include 1 John 4:7–8: "Beloved, let us love one another: for love is of God; and every one that loveth is born of God, and knoweth God. He that loveth not knoweth not God; for God is love."

We must boldly exist, not just subsist, in the love of Christ

---

We must boldly exist, not just subsist, in the love of Christ. We need to display it, wear it outwardly, and be a shining example. As Christians we present truths with crystal clarity, but if within our rhetoric there is no love, we are likened to 1 Corinthians 13:1: "Though I speak with the tongues of men and of angels, but have not love, I have become sounding brass or a clanging cymbal."

Our greatest witness is not the words we say—although we need to say the correct words. It is not the perfection of our theology—although our theology needs to be right. It is rather that we allow that theology to work in our lives, manifested in word and deed within the relationships we build with our fellow man—that's why it is called fellowship.

Our fellowship needs to move outward from our own comfort zone and small group of friends; it needs to encompass other Christians, other denominations, and yes, even those you might deem as non-believers as well. Jesus said, in John 10:16, "And other sheep I have, which are not of this fold: them also I must bring, and they will hear My voice; and there will be one flock, and one shepherd" (NKJV).

Christianity is not an exclusive club—it is all inclusive. Anything less is not fellowship—it's a clique. Jesus also called out the more "clique- oriented" in Matthew 23:13–14: "But woe unto you, scribes and Pharisees, hypocrites! for ye shut up the kingdom of heaven against men: for ye neither go in yourselves, neither suffer ye them that are entering to go in. Woe unto you, scribes and Pharisees, hypocrites! For ye devour widows' houses, and for a pretence make long prayer: therefore ye shall receive the greater damnation."

What is the greatest commandment? Remember what Matthew 22:37 tells us, "Love the LORD your God with all your heart, with all your soul, and with all your mind" (NKJV). And what was the second part again? Love your wife as you love yourself, right? Oh! My mistake—that's your neighbor you are supposed to love as you love yourself. All joking aside, though. The question is this: Is loving God just a feeling to make acknowledgment of His existence? What I mean is something like this, "Oh yeah, I know there's a God, He's out there somewhere."

Do I love my wife merely agreeing that she exists by having nice feelings about her—just sometimes? And I could do that … disrespect her, abuse her, lie to her, betray her, and treat her with disregard and contempt. Couldn't I feel attached to her sometimes and yet not love her? Yeah, I could try, but she wouldn't put up with that and I know that for certain.

Clearly love that exists only in our feelings and intellect is a worthless love. Love is an **action word** based on free will. Not a love that is selfish, convenient to whim or feeling, or reduced to an act that we commit to because it only makes us feel good. It should be a free and willful act even when we don't feel emotionally connected or rewarded by the endeavor. That is true love. It is the only way I can be sure that my love for my wife is actual love for her, rather than a love based on how she makes me feel. Through the times of good, bad, and indifference, that kind of love—a willful, active love—stands the test of time.

If we can all agree that our love for another human must function this way—or at least that it functions at all—how can we think that our love for Jesus should be any less? How can we think we are saved simply by acknowledging God's existence as we ignore Him, dismiss Him, betray Him, hate Him, and never bother to repent all our evil because we think our simple affirmation of His cosmic presence gives us entitlement to salvation?

That's not love, and it certainly is not belief or faith—that is downright blasphemy.

So, we all want to be good Christians. Let's look at what Christ went through on our behalf.

I can imagine the scene, with one Pharisee talking to another, pointing at Jesus…

"He's not one of us, you know. He's not even from around here. What good could possibly come out of Nazareth? He claims such a lofty position, yet we know the names of His parents. How is it that He knows so much about our business? He's uneducated and not refined like us … see how He's dressed. Look at who it is that are drawn to Him. Not one of those vile sinners have ever set foot inside of the synagogues is my guess. Actually, I personally wouldn't want them there, anyway…

"This Son of Man, as He calls Himself, mingles with sinners, publicans, and whores. It seems like He doesn't care about their wickedness. He certainly doesn't follow our ways or our methods of teaching. If he were a true prophet, He would harmonize with us and would treat that rabble with the indifference they deserve. Yet He treats them as little children.

"You know it angers me to see all those who have shown us nothing but contempt sitting there, giving their undivided attention to this Man they call the Messiah, the Christ. Something needs to be done about this before it gets out of hand. What do you think?"

Ecclesiastes 1:9: "The thing that hath been, it is that which shall be, and that which is done is that which shall be done: and there is no new thing under the sun."

2016 was a deadly year for being a Christian according to the Center for the Study of Global Christianity, which monitors worldwide demographic trends. Around 90,000 Christians were killed for their faith reported ABC News. Of course Christians are in daily danger in the middle eastern countries of Iran, Pakistan, Iraq, and Syria. North Korea, China, and India also have low tolerance levels for Christianity. Did you know that 80% of the people in this country claim to be Christians? (ABC news analysis by Gary Langer, July 18, 2001). How many do you think will find out that just maybe their claims might not hold up to the ultimate test?

This culture of ours is perfectly designed to lead us into complacency and a false faith. It's easy to be a Christian in the USA by popular standards, which is just a collection of friendly "let's feel good" sentiments. One is very apt to believe he is whatever the world considers him. Look, there is a Jesus fish sticker on that family's bumper … must be a Christian; there's a Bible quote on that person's Facebook® page and also look, there's one on another's Twitter® profile … yup, must be. Look at all those lovely Christmas lights … yessiree, must be a Christian. And as far as they are considered and how they think, they must be, too.

Our American culture is hostile to authentic Christianity.

Our American culture is hostile to authentic Christianity. Superficially a Christian in the USA can profit immensely (think of all the "Bling Pastors"), but a true faith may cost you. We are lucky—for the majority of us safely worshipping here under the stars and stripes it is just the occasional sarcastic, snide remark or a pouty face ... no threats here ... our livelihoods are not threatened too much. We are not spat upon, our clothes are not gambled for, and no thorns placed upon our heads, and our backs have not been scourged. And we haven't experienced total social alienation—yet. Let's check in on how it's going with Jesus.

The rabbinic view of Jesus concerning His relationship with the common people of the day put them in direct conflict with Him. Christ's mingling with the lowliest, rag-tag sinners displeased the Jewish hierarchy.

What did Jesus think about that? Those who regard themselves the favorites of heaven should know this. Jesus said, "My mission is not with you who are holy and righteous. The poor souls who feel their poverty and sinfulness ... these are the ones I have come to rescue. Angels in heaven are interested in the lost souls, those who are despised."

Romans 3: 11–12 shares, "There is none that understandeth, there is none that seeketh after God." They are all gone out of the way. Salvation does not come from our seeking after God. Rather our salvation comes from Jesus seeking us. What did Jesus say to Matthew? "Follow me ... And it came to pass, as Jesus sat at meat in the house, behold, many publicans and sinners came and sat down with Him and His disciples" (Matt. 9:9, 10). And the Pharisees asked the disciples, "Why eateth your master with publicans and sinners?" (Matt. 9:11). Now that was the question. The light of Christ's goodness was a sign post. Isaiah 30:21 tells us, "This is the way, walk ye in it," but the Pharisees choked at the thought and turned their questions instead towards the disciples, hoping to fuel the doubt they knew already existed to shake their weak faith. They aimed their arrows of shame, where they knew it would do the most harm. The Pharisees' intent was to shame Jesus and divide the disciples from each other and from their Teacher.

Who can say they've stood starving, utterly alone in the wilderness? Christ did and endured assaults from all sides, with no one to come to His defense and no one to tell Him how brave and awesome He was for standing up to the challenge, and for us no less. This situation rarely presents itself to us, but if it did and we endured, we can always hop on Facebook® and brag of our persecution in hopes of likes and shares.

Today it does not require great sacrifice to carry the Christian banner in America, as it does in Iraq or Libya or wherever else Christianity is being stoned. But if it did, would we still wave our banners in the breeze? If there was no chance of gaining any temporal reward for piety, would we bother? If proclamation of faith meant suffering and persecution, would we proclaim it?

If we wouldn't, then that flag of faith is merely a fashion statement. Sometimes we drape it over ourselves for our own sake … entirely artificial. Look out now! Once again we will refer to Matthew 23:13: "Woe to you, scribes and Pharisees, hypocrites!" Jesus, in Matthew 23, speaks to the disciples and the multitude. In verse 2 Jesus says, "The scribes and Pharisees sit in Moses' seat" **BUT** in verses 3 to 7 it shows us they put on the show just to be called Rabbi. "Even so ye outwardly appear righteous unto men, but within ye are full of hypocrisy and iniquity" (Matt. 23:28). Let's also read Matthew 23:23–24 where Jesus tells them that they "strain at the gnat but swallow a camel." What is Jesus suggesting? While condemning all the little nit-picky things they condemn themselves, but how and to what extent? Shaming and not forgiving—if you cannot forgive and include grace and mercy, how then can God do the same for you? Love is the key and Christ is love. If we do not feed the hungry, help the widows … show grace and kindness to our neighbors … Jesus will say, "I know you not."

The world beats us down, constantly testing us in one way or another, sometimes when the world can't break us there is the blame and shame game. The trickster throws us an outside curve ball just to see if we will chase after it. Well, Jesus could see it coming and knocked it out of the park. In John 8:3–11 a mob brought a woman who was caught in the act of adultery and threw her half naked into the dirt in front of Jesus. In this scenario they were tempting Jesus in order for them to shame and accuse Him. But as they pushed for a judgment call, Jesus remained calm and simply wrote into the dust with His finger many of the accuser's own sins, and He asked the question. "He that is without sin among you, let him first cast a stone at her" (vs. 7). From oldest to the youngest, the stones could be heard falling to the ground. They must have all swallowed their camels at that point, turned around, and left. As Jesus and the woman stood there all alone, He asked, "Where are those thine accusers? hath no man condemned thee?" (vs. 10). "No one," was her reply and Jesus said, "Neither do I condemn thee: go, and sin no more" (vs. 11). FORGIVENESS, MERCY, AND GRACE—**WITHOUT SHAME!**

Oh, I can hear the Pharisees now talking to the leaders of the mob they sent out. "What! We give you a simple task in order to entrap the Man and you can't even do that right? He is gaining popularity among the people and we hear their murmurings. When Christ cometh will he do more miracles then this man hath done? We must take him now! Send out the officers and pick him up." Said Jesus unto them, "Yet a little while am I with you, and then I go unto him that sent me. Ye shall seek me, and shall not find me: and where I am, thither ye cannot come" (John 7:33–34).

How many there are who hear the word of truth, but hate the message and the messenger, because the truth disturbs them in their deceptive practices.

John 8:25–30: "Then said they unto Him, Who art thou? And Jesus said unto them, Even the same that I said unto you from the beginning. I have many things to say and to judge of you: but he that sent me is true; and I speak to the world those things which I have heard of him. They understood not that he spake to them of the Father. Then said Jesus unto them, When ye have lifted up the Son of man, then shall ye know that I am He, and that I do nothing of myself; but as my Father hath taught me, I speak these things. And he that sent me is with me: the Father hath not left me alone; for I do always those things that please him. As he spake these words, many believed on him."

Two classes are plainly brought to view in these prior passages—the children of light, who hear and obey the truth, and the children of darkness, who reject the truth

Satan uses many tactics to move our attention away from Jesus. He instills in our hearts and minds untruths and twists our reality into believing there is sin where none exists. And that sin is punishable in this life, which then makes it appear that disease and death proceed from God as punishment arbitrarily inflicted on account of sin. The way was paved by this misunderstanding for the Jews to reject Jesus. He who, "hath borne our griefs and carried our sorrows" was looked upon as "stricken, smitten of God, and afflicted" (Isa. 53:4) and they hid their faces from Him (vs. 3).

Let's review the story of the man born blind in John 9. The disciples asked Jesus, "Who sinned? This man or his parents, for him to be born like that?" They did not understand, and Jesus gently explained to them that he was born such so that "the works of God should be made manifest in him" (vs. 3). As the man who was blind went about his way, people seemed confused, asking each other is this not the person who sat by the roadside begging? "It looks like he," they thought, "but how can a person who was blind all his life now see?" (vs. 18). But he clarified to all that a man called Jesus had healed him. He was brought to Pharisees, who could focus not on the miracle of his healing, but chose instead to condemn Jesus for healing on the Sabbath: "Therefore said some of the Pharisees, This man is not of God, because he keepeth not the sabbath day. Others said, How can a man that is a sinner do such miracles? And there was a division among them" (vs. 16).

They didn't believe him and called in the parents for proof. His parents were afraid of expulsion from the synagogue and were cautious with their answers. The parents verified that he was born blind but who performed the miracle they could not say. "Our son is of age," they told the Pharisees, "Why not ask him? He is not a mute and can speak for himself" (vs. 20, 21).

Then again they called the man who was blind back in for more questions in an attempt to trap him. At this point they wanted the man to deny Jesus and give God the praise, for they claimed that Jesus was a sinner. The man said that he did not know whether Jesus was a sinner or not, but he added, "Whereas I was blind, now I see" (vs. 25).

One more time they asked for an explanation. I would suggest that you open your Bible and read John 9:27–38 for the rest of the story. And for an even more fulfilling study, add to your reading the following:

Romans 10: 8–11: We shall not, nor ever should we, be ashamed about knowing Jesus.

Luke 13: 10–17: How can we be ashamed about knowing Jesus? By not doing what we have been called to do.

Philippians 2:5–11: With humility and by service we shall minister as Jesus did in order to complete and fulfill His ministry on earth.

Let us all take our fellowship through the ministry of Jesus Christ and complete the task of making God's kingdom on earth.

A modern-day saint's club fellowships with those who are spiritually good. Really? We need to be a rehab facility that wishes to fellowship with those who are spiritually needy. A greeter at the door may say to himself,

"Oh my, look at this one coming here. How can I allow them to fellowship with us?"

It should be, "Oh wow, this person looks like they are in so much need of fellowship. The love of Jesus needs to be poured out to them."

I was attending a seminar one evening and there was a teenage boy there who was attending as well. I was so glad that he took the invitation. He was struggling with his insecurity and age and I had known about him for some time and knew that he had to muster everything he had spiritually to be there. There was a pretty, young teenage girl who was further along in her spiritual walk attending as well, and made an effort to sit by this young man every chance she got. At the break she sat with him at one of the refreshment tables.

After the intermission we all went back to the seminar. However, the young man and the young lady were not seated.

Fifteen minutes went by and I heard a commotion coming from the hall. Apparently there were suspicions about where the two teens had gone and what they may or may not have been up to.

I heard an answer from the young lady stating, "We just went for a walk!

There's nothing going on except in your minds!"

Suggestions of impropriety were being tossed around as the grandparents of the young lady were on the defense, too.

The young man claimed no error, no foul. The whole thing was blown way out of proportion and the end result? Embarrassment of unfounded accusations and neither teen ever returned to fellowship. Let he who is without sin cast the first accusation…

There's sometimes little recognition of the needs of the people who, for whatever reason, have found their way through the doors of our church. At that very moment we need to take the opportunity to extend our hands in the manner of love. For reasons unknown at times we blow it; we deem ourselves judge and jury, sentencing our misunderstood guests, who include down-and-outers, strugglers, and those who have not yet arrived to the high standards demanded by our exclusive religious club. Woe is us who find it more necessary to protect our "fraternal order for the perfect," than to allow the lost sheep into the fold. Fellowship in the love that is Christ Jesus is the only thing that saves souls.

CHAPTER 8

In the Spirit—The Promise Fulfilled

Acts 2:1–3 tells us, "And when the day of Pentecost was fully come, they were all with one accord in one place. And suddenly there came a sound from heaven as of a rushing mighty wind, and it filled all the house where they were sitting. And there appeared to them cloven tongues like as of fire, and it sat upon each of them."

The time had now come. The Spirit had been waiting for the crucifixion, resurrection, and ascension of Christ. For ten days the disciples offered their petitions for the outpouring of the Spirit, and Christ in heaven added His intersession. This was the occasion of His ascension and inauguration—a jubilee in heaven. He had ascended on high, leading captivity captive, and He now claimed the gift of the Spirit, that He might pour it out upon His disciples (White, *Southern Watchman*, Nov. 28, 1905).

God is willing to give us a similar blessing, when we seek for it as earnestly. The reservoir of the heavenly Spirit is not locked up and hidden away for exclusive use—the Comforter is ours as well.

For the consecrated worker of God, wherever he may be, the Holy Spirit abides. The words spoken to the disciples hold true for us as well as we share the Holy Comforter. The Spirit furnishes the strength that sustains striving, lifting up souls in every emergency, wherever the hatred of the world invades, and within reflection of one's own failures and mistakes. In sorrow and affliction, where outlook seems darkest and with uncertain future, when we feel helpless and alone—these are the times when, in answer to the prayer of faith, the Holy Spirit brings comfort to the heart (White, *Acts of the Apostles*, p. 51).

In John 16:7–9, and 13, Jesus is speaking: "Nevertheless I tell you the truth; It is expedient for you that I go away: for if I go not away, the Comforter will not come unto you; but if I depart, I will send him unto you. And when he is come, he will reprove the world of sin, and of righteousness, and of judgment: Of sin, because they [the world] believe not on me ... Howbeit when he, the Spirit of truth, is come, he will guide you into all truth: for he shall not speak of himself; but whatsoever he shall hear, that shall he speak: and he will show you things to come."

It was a gift unequaled that Christ gave to us as He ascended from this earth. This gift was for all those who believed on Him, and those who should believe on Him. It was the gift needed to be worthy of His greatness and His royalty. He determined that gift would be His representative, the third person of the Godhead. This gift could not be excelled. He would give all gifts in one, and therefore the divine Spirit, that converting, enlightening, and sanctifying power, would be His donation.

In the flesh Christ was not ubiquitous and He needed to be in a position where He could accomplish the most important work by few and simple means. The plan of salvation is comprehensive, but its parts are few, and each part depends on the others, while all work together with utmost simplicity and in entire harmony. Christ is represented by the Holy Spirit, and when this Spirit is appreciated, when those controlled by the Spirit communicate to others the energy with which they are imbued, an invisible chord is touched which electrifies the whole. We all need to recognize and understand how boundless the energy is and vast the divine resources are which are readied for our call (White, *Southern Watchman*, Nov. 8, 1905).

The power ready to be given by God is a free gift for those who ask and who are willing to share that power, out of love, with others.

Consider, on the other hand, the story of Simon in Acts 8:14–24. The gift of the Holy Spirit cannot be purchased:

Now when the apostles which were at Jerusalem heard that Samaria had received the word of God, they sent unto them Peter and John: Who, when they were come down, prayed for them, that they might receive the Holy Ghost: (For as yet he was fallen upon none of them: only they were baptized in the name of the Lord Jesus.) Then laid they their hands on them, and they received the Holy Ghost. And when Simon saw that through laying on of the apostles' hands the Holy Ghost was given, he offered them money, Saying, give me also some of this power, that on whomsoever I lay hands, he may receive the Holy Ghost. But Peter said unto him, Thy money perish with thee, because thou hast thought that the gift of God may be purchased with money. Thou hast neither part nor lot in the matter: for thy heart is not in the sight of God. Repent therefore of this thy wickedness, and pray God, if perhaps the thought of thine heart may be forgiven thee. For I perceive that thou art in the gall of bitterness, and in the bond of iniquity. Then answered Simon, and said, Pray ye to the Lord for me, that none of these things which ye have spoken come upon me.

The Holy Spirit is there to convict and guide us as we unpack the gift of salvation. We need to take careful note as we proceed on our spiritual path to make sure that we follow certain procedures—read daily our Bible and commune early every day with the Divine Creator. In prayer, before the cross, ask for guidance.

The Day Our World Stood Still ...

It was springtime in the year 2007, and I was sitting in the office at my home in Mansfield, Texas. It was evening, and a storm had passed through the area ... perhaps it was a precursor to coming events? When my wife rushed into the room she was panic-stricken as she held out the phone to me. I had just finished a rewrite and I was drained. The look on her face was that of impending doom, "It's about Mom ... it's your sister-in-law!"

"Hello," I answered and listened to the unfolding of a very grim tale. "Mom's in a bad situation," my sister-in-law emphatically stated and added, "She has had a heart attack and they are trying to get her stabilized but are having a problem. They can't find the reason causing the trauma. It does not look good. I will call back in a few minutes ... they are calling us to come into the emergency area pronto."

After hanging up the phone my wife started demanding that I do something. "What are you talking about?" I asked. "We are helpless sitting here, and at the mercy of the ER where she has been taken for care. They are doing everything they possibly can, I'm sure."

The look on my wife's face was of unbelief and I know she felt the same desperation as I concerning our position. My suggestion at that moment was, "Let's pray."

RRRRIIIINNNNNG! I quickly took the call and it was the attending physician, who started explaining the problem to me. "It is not good, sir; we have brought your mother back three times so far from cardiac arrest, and we don't know what is causing this. We have no paperwork or directive, so it is our duty to resuscitate and keep trying to stabilize her in order to treat the symptom. We have administered a blood thinner in the hope at this time ... thinking it is a blockage ... I got to go ... they're calling me ... seems to be something more going on. I will call you back." ... CLICK!

I looked at the phone as an enemy and wanted to crush it into a million pieces. Oh how my heart ached as I saw my wife in tears ... "Whhaat?" she uttered. "What can we do?"

All I could do was to shake my head and say in a whisper, "It is in the Lord's hands, and we must take refuge in that."

All I could do was to shake my head and say in a whisper, "It is in the Lord's hands, and we must take refuge in that."

Looking at the clock I wanted to curse it as seconds merged into minutes and minutes trudged into a half hour. I was wringing my hands, grinding my teeth, waiting for a response—any response—from the stupid land line.

RRRRIIIIINNNNG! My wife reached for the phone, but I quickly snatched the receiver and placed my ear to the device and answered, "Hello?"

It was the doctor once again, and he seemed out of breath, but his tone was less dire. "We finally got her stabilized. She is a fighter, sir. She has gone through five cardiac arrests and we know what has caused this. She has several pulmonary embolisms and with the blood thinner it seems to have alleviated some of the stress on her heart. Understand she is not out of danger. We will be taking her to the ICU. I suggest that you call there in the morning for an update. I will put your relation on the phone now."

My sister-in-law's voice was next on the line, "Your brother chose to stay as close as possible to Mom, so I guess the doctor told you everything that is going on. If she makes it through the night, perhaps you guys should consider coming up because we have to get all these legal issues straightened out anyway. We thought for sure there was a directive somewhere because Mom said to us that if her quality of life deteriorates to an unacceptable point that she wanted to be let go."

"I know, too, that is what she would have wanted," I said and added, "I will call the ICU first thing and we will make plans to fly up there."

Once again, my wife and I petitioned the Lord for the betterment of Mom's dilemma and for guidance on how to proceed. Morning could not come soon enough. First we called the hospital ICU to find out that Mom was hanging in there but the nurse warned me, "Sir, if you want to see your mother alive I suggest that you get here as soon as you possibly can. That's just my advice, as this can go any direction at this point."

As I was making phone inquiries my wife was making plane reservations. Next on my list was a call to my brother to discuss what we needed to do concerning Mom and how to proceed with her recovery.

My brother answered, "Well, I guess you know Mom made it through the night. So now what do we do? You're the elder so what is your suggestion?" "Quality of life," I said, "Is what we must think about for her."

"I agree," my brother replied. "I thought Mom and Dad had a directive of quality of life made up by their attorney? I will call them to see where it is if it exists."

"Good idea," I added, "Since she is now being kept alive by the machines, maybe because of everything she's been through ... and don't take this the wrong way ... we have to ask the question of what will be her quality of life?"

My brother answered, "There's no shame in asking or considering what is best for our mother. God, I know you weren't there last night, but we were, and it was hell seeing them coming and going, putting up the fight for Mom. It was all I could do to be there; we knew we had to stay until it was over or not."

"I'm sorry you went through that, man," I said. "So she is on life support ... the only way we will know about her true condition is to gradually remove the machines."

"If you are in agreement with that, then I think that is what we need to do as well," my brother stated and then added, "I will call over to the ICU and tell them that is what we want to do. We will be heading over there around four this afternoon. I'll call you after that."

After hanging up the phone my wife and I again sent out our petitions to the Great Physicians—God our Father, His Son Jesus Christ, and the Holy Spirit.

Our plane flight was a midnight, red-eye express with an early morning arrival, and Lord willing, we should get to the hospital sometime between 9–10 am, Eastern time.

Four o'clock came and went, and at five the phone rang. It was my brother calling with the update, "We arrived at the ICU around three and the nurse asked us to remain in the waiting area. The doctor came out and told us that they did as asked and removed the life support. Her temperature increased to normal, her color came back, and now she is breathing on her own. Then he asked us to come with him to see if she is cognizant. So we followed him to where Mom was resting. He said that if she is responsive she would not be able to speak because of the breathing tubes that were in her mouth and esophagus. The doctor went to look in her eyes with a light and before he touched her ... she opened her eyes. It was like she knew he was there. We asked if she knew who we were and she nodded her head yes. We told her to blink her eyes once for yes and twice for no as we knew she could not speak. We asked if she knew what happened and she blinked twice. We told her what happened and asked if she knew where she was and so she looked around and blinked once. Anyway, that's what happened, and they will send her to the observation floor tomorrow morning, which is on the third floor. Have you guys made reservations?"

First I said, "That is an amazing story. It is truly a miracle and we are headed that way and will arrive sometime in the morning."

Once in Baltimore we rented a car and headed north, meeting our predicted schedule.

Upon arrival I first met with the doctor in charge and he confirmed that there was no procedural letter for quality of life anywhere to his knowledge and he was obligated to follow standard insurance guidelines to treat Mom's condition. I then made a phone call to my brother and he had no evidence, either, of an existing directive document.

Okay, so what do we do? We have to ask Mom how she wants to proceed. My wife went into Mom's room and there she was—eyes closed, not much color, and fighting for each breath, gurgling through a mass of mucous. Frankly speaking, I was shocked and started to wonder, *is this the insurance standard the leading physician was talking about?* Touching Mom's arm, there was no response, no flutter of the eyes that my brother had spoken about, and her skin felt clammy. With my blood pressure on the rise I began to look for answers, and my first stop was the nurse's station at the end of the hall.

Who is in charge of taking care of our mother was my request. I was introduced to a lady who was dressed according to the standard new, happy attire nurses wear these days—a one color blue top with matching

Elmo® fleece pants and sneakers. (Please note that I praise these nurses for doing one of the most thankless jobs imaginable.)

My request to the head nurse was, "We need to be able to speak with our mother. She appears unresponsive. There seems to be an unusual amount of phlegm inhibiting her breathing and her ability to communicate—is there anything that you can do?"

I received an unsatisfactory response. "Sir, I understand your concern, but we have done everything required to keep your mother comfortable. When we try to suction out the mucous, she bites down on the instrument, not letting us do our job."

Biting my tongue, I took a deep breath, paused, and politely asked, "Ma'am, I have traveled a long way, and I am sure you have indeed done everything possible at this juncture to keep my mother comfortable. I would be further in your debt if you would be so kind to try again. You see, it is imperative that we communicate with her as there appears to be no directive. Communication is the only way to avoid her becoming a statistic of a corporative procedure rather than to gain some hope of having any quality of life. So do you think you could help us out here?"

As I searched the nurse's eyes she then said, "We will try again to see if we can be of help."

I smiled and said, "Thank you. I am sure that we will have success." With that being said, I turned and went down the steps to the prayer garden, and it was the first of many such journeys that day. Well-wishers faded in and out. Their thoughts and prayers were said over our still-unresponsive mother. Back to the prayer garden I went once again, with even more furtive supplications: "We need an angel, Lord—send us one of Your Holy Healing Angels."

With that being said, I turned and went down the steps to the prayer garden, and it was the first of many such journeys that day.

Upon entering the lobby of the hospital, I saw my wife, my cousin, and his wife in conversation. Approaching them I asked my cousin if they had been up to see Mom. They said they were waiting for my return.

Mom was still in the same condition—no better, no worse. The sun was going down and my cousin asked if we had something to eat. Accessing the fact that time seemed to have flown by and we had had nothing since we arrived, we turned to leave and were met by a young, blond lady. She was clothed head to toe in what I recall to this day as a proper, white nurses uniform, inclusive of even the stethoscope around her neck.

Making it her point she asked, "What seems to be your concerns?" I relayed all the history of the day's frustrations.

She smiled and said assuredly; "By the time you return from your meal your mother will be responsive and able to talk to you."

We didn't think much of it … just figured good! At last maybe here is someone who knows what they are doing. Perhaps at last indeed?

Lighting had been dimmed as hospital procedure required when we came back to the third-floor observation area. We peered into Mom's room, and there she was—her color was good and she seemed to be resting and breathing normally. From behind us a soft voice urged, "She is ready and will see you now. Go ahead; touch her arm."

I asked the nurse, "Because of our situation could you document our conversation with our mother?"

"Of course, I would be happy to do that," was the nurse's reply.

It seemed like we were the only ones in the entire hospital and all focus in the entire universe was resting on that tiny room.

Afraid to intrude on my mother's peaceful rest, I gently brushed her arm with my fingertips. Her eyes opened, and she smiled. My cousin was the first to speak, "Do you know who we are?"

Mom affirmed by naming each one of us. Then my cousin said, "When I was first introduced to you, I thought you were the most beautiful woman I had ever met."

This brought a subdued laugh from Mom as she whispered, "I don't look or feel so pretty right now."

Explaining to Mom that if she felt up to it we needed to ask some questions about what she wanted to see happen in the future pertaining to her health and where she wanted to go after this hospital stay was over.

"I want to get better and return to the retirement home if that's okay with everybody," Mom responded.

My mother was always thinking of everyone else, even at this time asking if it was okay. I was near to tears. "I know what happened, Mom, and I have been told that because of the Parkinson's the food sometimes goes down into your lungs. So they might have to put a feeding tube into your stomach," I explained to her.

"I am fine with that if it is needed," Mom said, agreeing with such a procedure.

After answering all the important questions and showing that she was lucid and able, Mom began to look tired. The nurse said she would put her notes at the nurses' station so when the morning shift came on it could be seen by the attending physician.

Relaying the message to my brother that the mission had been accomplished, he told me that he would check to make sure that the directive was filed. My wife and I returned home, and I called my brother the next day, inquiring as to Mom's condition. She been returned to the nursing home and he curiously told me that the description of the nurse who witnessed the directive seemed to not match any of the attending care givers that were on duty that evening. Blond hair, well-kept, blue eyes, wearing full and proper nursing attire—in this day and age?

Prayer is a powerful tool.

CHAPTER 9

The Kingdom Is Not Exclusive

Prayer being what it is, it must also be realized that if it is within His plan, it will be made manifest. Remember, the Creator is not a God of confusion; He is the same today as He was in Genesis. As it was in the days of Noah it still remains today. That being said, as I was looking for a closing chapter title and subject, I put it in prayer. I wanted this manuscript finished months ago, in my time. But there were no immediate answers, no brainiac moments, no signs or direction. BUT ... while on vacation in Florida, my family and I attended a very small and humble church. We were slightly on time and were greeted by the person delivering the morning Bible study. As I sat down, I began to absorb what was being delivered.

"Oh," the brother stated, "You want exclusivity? Well then go join the country club or one of those secret societies. Go ask the homeless person on the street if he feels included in life's abundancy. Go ask a battered mother how exclusive she feels. Go ask a drug addict who is one shot away from deaths door if he deems himself exclusive to, or included in, God's tender mercy. How about the unwed mother, now rejected by friends and family, so embarrassed by her mistake that she is afraid to even attend church? How included in what she remembers of life's normalcy is she now? No, she is excluded from the love she once knew and that which she relied upon for her familiar balance. This kind of rejection and exclusion from the love of Jesus Christ will send those in need running off light speed in the wrong direction. And where will they end up through their decisions made out of desperation?"

How lofty stand our church steeples … how high off the ground they appear and how out of touch are we to those standing firmly planted in earth's soil.

There is a story told of a young man who grew up with several disorders. First of all, he was dyslexic, but he also had an attention deficit problem. The young man strived to fit in, knowing that he was just a little different from other children. His parents raised him in the Christian faith and this young man showed the Lord's character whenever he was asked to help with a task—never said no, he was always willing.

In fact, knowing that he was somewhat challenged he chose after high school to join the military, just to prove that he could succeed. And succeed he did. In battle he saved many of his fellow soldiers during a fire fight against overwhelming odds.

But the stress of battle had a price and further manifested itself when he returned home. He was diagnosed with PTSD (Posttraumatic Stress Disorder). Outwardly the hurt doesn't show but the pain within still grows. He looked to family and church for help, but he no longer felt that he fit in anywhere.

While attending a men's prayer breakfast he went into shock and started shouting out in the middle of prayer time. Two deacons escorted him out of the church and told him that he had to be more in touch and in control of himself if he wanted to attend church functions. Really?

Maybe it was how they said it, or maybe it was how they treated him because he was different and had special needs. They never saw the veteran return. It was told that the soldier went into deep depression and at one point ended his own life.

It is so important that we take the words of Matthew 25:34–40 to heart:

Then shall the King say to them on his right hand, Come, ye blessed of my Father, inherit the kingdom prepared for you from the foundation of the world: For I was an hungered, and ye gave me meat: I was thirsty, and ye gave me drink: I was a stranger, and ye took me in: Naked, and ye clothed me: I was sick and ye visited me: I was in prison, and ye came unto me. Then shall the righteous answer him, saying, Lord, when saw we thee an hungered, and fed thee? or thirsty, and gave thee drink? When saw we thee a stranger, and took thee in? or naked, and clothed thee? Or when saw we thee sick, or in prison, and came unto thee? And the King shall answer and say unto them, Verily I say unto you, Inasmuch as ye have done it unto one of the least of these my brethren, ye have done it unto me.

It was an opportunity missed to show compassion and empathy to someone who gave much and received so little love and understanding. It happens—more often than we'd like to think—and we need be ashamed of such actions.

There is also a story of a young girl who grew up in a two-income, middle-class home. Her parents did not know the faith. The father paid little to no mind of his daughter and the mother worked long hours to help make the two ends meet.

The young girl found a job in a restaurant in the shadow of a church steeple. She watched people both young and old coming and going. Many would visit the eatery where she worked. Everyone from that church looked so friendly and there emitted from their glowing faces hope and a promise of a bright future.

The mirror revealed to her the desperation of passing years and she searched everywhere in the hope of her own better life. Try as she might, there were no Prince Charmings who stepped forward. There were only young men with hollow promises exchanged for her favor. When she tried to talk to her parents about life and future plans, she was met with, "Not now" or "I'm too busy" or dead ends.

One Sabbath she even tried to dress up to fit in and went to that church where everyone looked so friendly. When she entered though, she found the sanctuary cold as the dank autumn day that brought her there. They all seemed to be too busy—little bees buzzing around in their own little circles to note a care when she walked out.

In her pain she pondered their hypocrisy. She read over and crumbled up the little invitation cards and tracts they left on tables. "How can they not see me? Can they not hear my inner cry? How could they not have noticed me when I walked into their church? I have served them; I have waited on them. I smile and I am polite, and all the while my heart aches."

The waitress slumped into a chair and sighed, "Lord, am I that invisible?" Suddenly a hand gently brushed hers. She looked up and it was a young girl who returned for her purse. But this time was different and this time she was asked, "I see you ... how may I help?"

The Lord clearly sees us all. Though we are smitten by the human condition, tainted by human stain—frail, insecure, uncomfortable in our skin, bent and broken, He accepts us where we are. There is no exclusion because of race, creed, or color. His promises are for all kindred, tongues, and nationalities. Christ exudes a healing love without boundary or borders. The kingdom of Christ's church is the emergency room for all who are broken.

The Lord clearly sees us all. Though we are smitten by the human condition, tainted by human stain— frail, insecure, uncomfortable in our skin, bent and broken, He accepts us where we are.

Matthew 11:28–30 says, "Come unto me, **ALL** ye that labour and are heavy laden, and I will give you rest. Take my yoke upon you, and learn of me; for I am meek and lowly in heart: and ye shall find rest unto your souls. For my yoke is easy, and my burden light" (emphasis added).

Martin Luther said of this passage, "He invites us with the greatest kindness. Now it is surely a sin and a shame that He cordially and faithfully summons us and exhorts us to our highest and greatest good, and we act so distantly with regard to it, and permit so long a time to pass ... that we grow quite, cold and hardened, so that we have no inclination or love for it" (From *Luther's Large Catechism* by Martin Luther).

I take from what Luther has stated in that passage two things. First, it is a sin for Christians to ignore that which Christ has called upon us to do. If we don't exercise it, we will lose it. Secondly, remember it is also a sin to hide the invitation and not pass it forward, for all humanity is our business.

Christ in verse 28 of Matthew 11 says "ALL"—that is **everyone** that labours. Who does that exclude? Nobody! Who is included? Let's look at Matthew 28:19, "Go ye therefore, and teach all nations, baptizing them in the name of the Father, and of the Son, and of the Holy Ghost." And also Revelation 7:9: "After this I beheld, and, lo, a great multitude, which no man could number, of all nations, and kindreds, and people, and tongues, stood before the throne, and before the Lamb, clothed with white robes, and palms in their hands."

Matthew 11: 28 uses the term "labour" ... who does not labor? Everyone labors, and I believe that it implies worry. Who does not worry? No one person on earth is immune; at one time or another we are all laboriously worried and burdened with concern. The term "heavy laden" denotes a ship so filled to capacity that it is hard to steer and keep balanced. How often do we lose our sense of mental balance and the rudder of normalcy seems to be missing? Life's burdens become overwhelming—the flood gates of despair overcome us until at one point we cry out, "My Lord, my Lord, where art thou?"

However, take to heart and believe: "And the peace of God, which passeth all understanding, shall keep your hearts and minds through Christ Jesus" (Phil. 4:7).

Jesus is our friend: "Henceforth I call you not servants; for the servant knoweth not what his lord doeth: but I have called you friends;

for all things that I have heard of my Father I have made known unto you" (John 15:15).

Christ took it upon himself to redeem us with His blood: "And they sung a new song, saying, Thou art worthy to take the book, and to open the seals thereof: for thou wast slain, and hast redeemed us to God by thy blood out of every kindred, and tongue, and people, and nation" (Rev. 5:9).

"Forasmuch as ye know that ye were not redeemed with corruptible things, as silver and gold, from your vain conversation received by tradition from your fathers. But with the precious blood of Christ, as of a lamb without blemish and without spot" (1 Pet. 1:18, 19).

We are to be Christ's ambassadors: "Now then we are ambassadors for Christ, as though God did beseech you by us: we pray you in Christ's stead, be ye reconciled to God. For he hath made him to be sin for us, who knew no sin; that we might be made the righteousness of God in Him" (2 Cor. 5:20, 21).

Hey, you, with the tattoo … you with the body piercings … you with the purple hair and make-up … you who feel you are living a life not worthy of note … I am talking to you today.

Please allow me to relate to you another true story. I was in the music business for twenty-plus years and I have experienced most of what might be unpalatable to a normal lifestyle. This is a little excerpt from a few days of travel.

"Tiny," the Disciple from Arkansas …

As was his description of self, he was a gentle giant from the back hills of Arkansas, sent forth on a mission from God. He was as Larry noted, the height of a medium-sized Arkansas oak, the girth of an Amana® refrigerator, and built with the resiliency of a 1950 Studebaker. This soft- spoken, bushy-haired, bearded mountain man explained that he had the determination to go where other ministers rarely tread. He wanted to keep the company of the neediest life forms. This mindset brought him to a city in Michigan where he was hired as a bouncer in a night club. This drinking establishment was home to some of the roughest individuals. The biker bar held about a thousand patrons and some of the better bands on the A-club circuit provided the entertainment. Larry happened to be in one of those bands and that is how he met "Tiny."

But how did Larry come to be there, you might ask? Well, I am going to tell you. Let's back up the bus … set time to the year 1970. He was at the time recently divorced and a starving pilgrim; a "Useless Eater" by certain standards. The rock band he was a part of was attempting to shake the very foundation of the music world. Great expectations filled their minds and hearts, driving them towards the illusive dream of success. West was their destination and they readied for their first band road trip. The agent man booked three weeks—one club in Michigan, another in Chicago down the street from the Playboy Club, and another in the college town of Morgantown, West Virginia.

Lead singer Ed and Larry, the bass player, both full of salt and vinegar with no sleep, following a previous night's engagement, decided to press on and drive the equipment truck straight on to Michigan. Heading west on Interstate 80, the Pennsylvania sunrise was swiftly approaching their backside. At that time in their career the equipment truck consisted of a large bread van. It was very uncomfortable to drive, let alone having to be a passenger.

Riding shotgun on the fold-down utility seat, Larry considered trying to sleep. Too tired to think about what consequences would be later to his body, Larry caved in and cocooned into an old sleeping bag. The continual drone of the engine helped send him into semi-consciousness, as he lay wedged between the seat and the pocket door of the van.

At the top bread truck speed of 60 mph, the plan was that Larry would take the steering wheel after crossing the Ohio state line. Being jostled around and having head and spine glance off the door one too many times, Larry couldn't take it anymore and gave up the dream of sleep. Mental cobwebs gave way and vision began to clear. Behold, a beautiful Sunday morning appeared, enhanced by sunlight shimmering off the open road.

"Good to see you're up!" Ed yelled over the annoying engine noise. "I was bored to death without your company to keep me awake ... wouldn't want to fall asleep at the wheel!"

"Wouldn't want that ... yeah, I'm up if that's what you'd call it!" Larry screamed back. "Need to make an assessment of my body to see if I left any parts along the highway. Make a pit stop at the next exit and I'll take over driving. We're close to the state line."

"There's an exit coming up in about two miles," hollered Ed. "The sign said fuel and food, so that'll work!"

"Snow Shoe, exit one mile!" Larry called out.

Ed yelled back, "Thank goodness it's not snowing. And if it was, this would be an even more miserable trip! I don't like winter and I sure don't like traveling in it. Maybe we could play jobs in Florida during the ..."

Holding up his hand stopping Ed in mid-sentence, Larry said, "It's a rattling noise, Ed! Doesn't sound like general road noise." He was sounding desperate.

"What's the matter with you?" Ed questioned as he took the off ramp. "Something's making a weird sound," Larry warned and pointed, "noise coming from the right front ... heard this before ... can't remember when!" Ed slowed the truck even more and as he did the vibration got louder. "Waite a minute, Ed, I remember," shouted Larry. "That noise! ... Don't slow down! ... Keep your speed up!" The warning was too late.

Watching in horror, the two men saw the passenger's side front wheel fly off, spring into the air, and go bouncing out ahead of them. Sliding to a stop, shiny side up, the truck came to rest on the soft shoulder of the exit ramp.

Complexion paled, Ed sat cemented in his seat looking straight ahead. His fingers, white knuckled, were gripping the steering wheel. Slowly and silently he reached down and turned the ignition off. Irrationally pounding the steering wheel Ed yelled out, "I don't believe this ... did you see that ... we could have been killed or worse ... crushed by all this stupid equipment behind us!"

"Yeah," Larry said, "Maybe?"

"Maybe my aunt fanny," Ed blurted out, obviously irritated by the flip answer and continued with his observation. "If that wheel had come off traveling at sixty miles an hour, we would have been roadkill for sure. They could be peeling us off the interstate and tossing body parts into the meat wagon right now!"

"You see, Ed," Larry explained, "That wouldn't have happened. The speed of the wheel's turning motion, or the centrifugal force, held the wheel in place. Only by slowing down did it begin to lose cohesion and allowed us to hear the vibration and detect the problem. As we slowed further to make the turn onto the ramp the wheel released itself from its position on the hub and mount and away it went, *BOING*, flying into the air. I've seen this before in another situation."

Ed sat in the driver's seat in silence, patiently listening to Larry's monologue, but in apparent disbelief readied for rebuttal. "BOING! SITUATION YOU SAY ... are you nuts?" he asked. "I don't give a rat about how or why, just about the fact that it happened. You sound like ... so aloof to this problem ... like you are that guy, what's his name from Star Trek ... oh yeah, Spock."

"Sorry Ed," Larry apologized. "I didn't mean to come off like that. However, we are safe and sound, thanks be to God."

Sliding the passenger's door open Larry hopped out of the truck. Once on the ground he looked at the hub to see if it was damaged, and miraculously like the two boys, it was in good condition. Larry called out to his travel partner, "You gonna just sit there, or what?"

Finally Ed unhooked, got out of the truck to have a look, gave a whistle, and stated, "Very fortuitous, L. B., that's all I can say, very fortuitous. Two lucky dudes are we ... very fortunate, indeed."

"Maybe you think yourself a lyricist," Larry quipped.

Laughing, Ed pointed towards the end of the ramp. "Right now, looky there, why don't we get our lucky selves up to the end of this ramp?"

There was a garage located at the top of the hill, less than fifty yards away. The sign above two large roll-up doors read *Road Service and Truck Repairs* ... it was indeed a bright, bright sunshiny day.

Bread van, equipment, and passengers eventually rolled safely to Michigan. As the duo entered the night club, eyes adjusted to the dim light and focused on "Tiny," the gentle giant from Arkansas. Coming forward, he offered out his hand and introduced himself and his friend Dave as the bouncers for the club. If Tiny was a gallon jug, Dave was a half pint. But Dave held a second-degree black belt in Korean Karate. Together they made an awesome team when it came to crowd control. This was something to witness and would be appreciated later by the band.

Tiny demanded, "Belly up to the bar over there, shake off the road dirt, and relax before unloading the truck."

"What'll you have?" Dave asked.

Ed opted for a beer.

Larry said, "I'll do fine with a glass of milk."

Dave looked at Tiny, Tiny back at Dave, and they both looked at Larry like he suddenly sprouted two heads. "What ... you can't be serious!" Dave exclaimed.

"Come on man ... you're a rock'n rolla and you can't have a drink with the boys?" Tiny asked.

"Nervous stomach," Ed said rubbing his mid-section. "Very rare that he drinks. Go figure ... he still rocks."

Smiling, Dave assured Larry that he would fix him right up. Reaching down into a cooler, Dave pulled out a half gallon of milk, sat up a pint glass, and filled it up. "There ya go buddy," he said, "Just so you don't feel left out!"

"So, Tiny ... you are from Arkansas and I see that you didn't take a shot either," Larry said and then asked, "So what brought you, to of all places, this city in Michigan?"

Looking at Tiny, Dave prodded him to explain. "You guys ain't gonna believe this one, but go ahead, big guy, give them the one-hundred dollar round tour of *All About Tiny.*"

Tiny took a deep breath and drawled out, "Ooookaaay ... It's all about the dynamics of physics ... the natural order of things." The large-framed man patted his chest and continued, "For every action there comes an equal and opposing reaction ... now that all makes sense to you fellers, don't it?"

"Yeah, sure ... that all seems to make sense," Ed answered.

"Good," Tiny stated, "Then I shall begin my story ... I am an ordained Baptist Minister," he confessed, and as he said that, eyebrows of both Ed and Larry raised to the ceiling.

Tiny put up his hands and spoke, "I know ... I know, that sounds crazy to you two, but let me explain. It was an explosion that lifted me to where I stand today. Not just a physical one, but a spiritual one as well. It was late at night," he continued, "Roads were slick from a thunder storm, and I was driving home from a revival meeting. My flock, or church if you will, was in a little town located just outside of Hot Springs."

Toasting Tiny with a shot of milk Larry urged him on, "Please continue with the story."

"With your permission then," Tiny stated, eyeballing Larry. "As I said, roads were slick and wind-driven drizzle made visibility poor. Approaching an intersection, I saw the light turn green. And I didn't slow down. While passing under the light, life as I knew it evaporated. I thought a bomb went off ... light faded to black. That is my recollection prior, the next time I was cognizant was in the hospital. That in a nutshell is the action that brought me to "The Zoo," as we call it."

"Okay, Tiny," Ed said, "I understand the physical but let's hear about the spiritual."

"Yeah," agreeing with Ed, Larry asked, "Has to be more to the story ... fill in the blanks ... you're in the hospital, now what? I notice you have a slight limp. From what you are alluding to, that must have been some kind of accident, not just for physical reasons—something else uprooted you from a retreat to imbed you in a world of concrete and steel?"

Tiny gave a wink from under his bushy hair and said, "Yup, you're right. It was a spiritual awakening for me. Everybody's usually from somewhere's else ... right? And me ... I'm just an old billy from Arkansas. As I told ya, I had a calling there as a minister ... but it was a rebel yell that brought me here. Could have remained at the sleepy country church—to do that I would have been living a lie, been lying to my church, but most important ... I would have been denying God."

Pouring of libations continued as Tiny kept talking, "There was a hard- working, truck-driving good old boy who was part of our flock. But like so many, he slipped away from grace for a while. Rather than go home to his wife and kids he chose to go out carousing with the boys. He spent his truck driving earnings on cheap booze and women. Sure, he knew better, but the old devil snatched him up out on that long, lonely highway and tossed him to the gutter side of life.

The two musicians sat enthralled, truth-be-told, listening to Tiny's odd story, and Larry said, "There's got to be an unwritten song in this somewhere."

"Probably a country song," Tiny said, and continued, "Old Jake, as I will call him, was drinking with the boys at Slim Jim's Tavern one evening after coming off the road from a long haul—Little Rock to L.A. and back again. Instead of going straight home, Jake took a detour over to Slim's for a few cold ones and to see who was hangin' out. Slim's always had live music cranking and that Saturday night was no different. By the time Jake left that fine drinking establishment, he was three sheets to the wind and gone with a *not so ladylike* hangin' off his arm. He and his new passenger crawled into his beautiful new Kenworth he had mortgaged his family home to purchase. Bobtailing ... off he went—he wasn't going straight home. No, not when the little devil was doin' the thinkin'.

"I can just see Jake eying his new friend's legs in the dim light as she had her feet propped up on the truck dash. There he was watching the road and feeding his great expectations as he looked over at those pair of waiting arms. Back and forth went old Jake's eyes ... from the road to that skirt and back again. That was about the time Kenworth the truck was introduced to Lincoln the car.

"EXPLOSION ... a whole lot of smashing and mashing took place as his truck t-boned my car's passenger side. Toppling over a light pole and clipping a fire hydrant, the force of the impact pushed me, car, and the whole mess through the plate glass front window of a pharmacy."

"And you are miraculously alive to tell the tale!" Larry shouted. Ed gave out a long whistle and said, "I'm here to testify that fact." "He is ... larger than life," Dave concurred, hoisting a glass!

Placing his right hand heavenward, Tiny raised his voice, "Thank you, Lord, that I am still here, and I can tell about Your miracles!"

"Thank you, Lord, that I am still here, and I can tell
about Your miracles!"

The new believers asked for the story—the whole story—so help them God, that they should receive with no deleted chapter or verse.

Obligingly Tiny moved on as every good preacher does, "What the good Lord provided was a rain slicked highway and the fact the Lincoln was built like a Sherman tank. There was no cheap, thin sheet metal on that ride. Even out of such misfortune we see that God always has a plan and is watching over His flock. Amen."

All seated at the bar agreed, "Amen."

"Upon waking up," Tiny went on, "the original attending physician was there. He told me I was on the shady side of life when I was brought in. He held out his hand, and in it the good doctor held the radio antenna from the Lincoln. Believing that I would want to keep it as a souvenir he had cleaned it up so I could take it along home upon release.

Somehow, from what the doctor told me, I ended up outside the vehicle, unconscious on the floor of the pharmacy. My left leg was broken, my left arm as well, and I had multiple head contusions and a concussion. The paramedics found me underneath store shelving, but the oddity was a car radio antenna had found a home poking a way right through my mid- section. I explained to the doc that I was thinking of going on a diet. He told me that it was because of my girth and mass that the antenna didn't hit any vitals when it skewered my body. You see by this, God's plan is infallible, above reproach, and without question."

Dave raised his glass ... Ed took another shot as Larry pounded down the remaining half pint of milk.

"My friends," Tiny explained, "The hair wasn't long at that time, and the face clean shaven, and I was not as heavy, nor did I wear bib overalls. Back then, I wore a Brooks Brother's suit, a tie, and Bostonians. I was content, I might add, to preach the Gospel in the small country church. As you can see by the look of me now ... obviously that's all changed."

"That's for sure, and then some," Larry blurted out.

"After the hospital experience," Tiny stated, and again eyeballing Larry, "Relating to people what my new calling would be ... they thought me a nut. Having a whole bunch of down time to think, my thinkin' was that I needed to make huge changes. God saved me for a reason and I figured I was now personally on His mission. When He speaks boys ... you had better listen and understand what He says. So pray without ceasing, fellas. Psalm 22:11 says, 'Be not far from me; for trouble is near; for there is none to help.'"

"Amidst all the chaos," Tiny assured, "lives were saved and I am not just talkin' about the physical lives that were spared. Jake came to talk to me after everything was all over ..."

"He lived, too?" Ed interrupted, asking in disbelief.

"Unreal," Larry mumbled. "Hey, what about the babe riding shotgun?" "Oh, yes," Tiny said. "She was spared, and a downtrodden Jake came to

me and begged for forgiveness. As far as I was concerned, I told him he was already forgiven, but I wanted him to do something for himself and his family."

"Anything," Jake said to me. "Ask me and it's yours."

"'Jake,' I said to him, 'You need to get saved yourself—the accident was a wake-up call. The Lord gave you a second chance ... don't waste it.' Jake heeded the call and accepted Christ as his Lord and Savior. He went on his knees to his wife and children begging forgiveness. Jake became an integral part of the church and is now a faithful follower—

and no more long- haulin'. He's making sure that each week his whole family is there in church right beside him.

"He has taken his ministry to the road, testifying to all he comes into contact with about his fall into darkness and his rise through grace to now walk in the light of Jesus. What a powerful turn around and testimony Jake has, my friends. Out there on the lonesome highway he is known as; 'CB Jake Truckin' for Jesus.' As it is said in Psalm 19:14, 'Let the words of my mouth, and the meditation of my heart, be acceptable in thy sight, O LORD, my strength, and my redeemer.'"

This was all news to Ed, and Larry didn't know whether to ask for a hall pass to the toilet or go blind at that point. This was so out of character to listen to a minister give testimony ... but in a barroom, no less? Larry had a brain cramp and troubled himself about wrapping logic around this discourse ... and he wasn't even drinking. But if he was, he deemed this would be the calling to stop.

After about a minute of silence, "It doesn't stop there," Tiny cautioned, "Oh no ... I told Jake like I saw it ... the accident was a blessing to me. And when I told him that ... whoa, he like came unglued."

"Jake said to me, 'You must be insane!'

"I said, to the contrary, I gained my sanity and I was not going on a diet! No-ssiree ... the Lord blessed me with size and stature ... and that's what saved my life. I then told him that I was not going to pastor the church anymore ... need to go where the sinners are.

"Jake looked at me, and said, 'Well, John, you are a minister ... of course you need to go where the sinners are ... but there are sinners right here.'

"That's where I stopped him in mid-sentence. I paused ... looked Jake straight in the eye and said, 'Jake my name isn't John anymore. God gave me a new name ... it is Tiny.' I could see a strange, faraway look in Jake's eyes and he was a little taken back by my claim. So, I dropped that subject and assured him that he could still know me as John. He said that was good because there was only so much an old steel horse cowboy could handle at one time.

"After all that drama boys ... I am exactly where the good Lord wants me to be!"

Raising his hand, Larry questioned, "Where might that be, Tiny?"

Faster than a hot rod Lincoln the big man adeptly hustled from behind the bar, grabbed Larry, put him in a head lock, knuckled the top of his head, and said, "Like I said—right here bangin' hard-headed heathens like you through these metal fire doors, throwing their drunken, sinful spirits out onto the street. All the while I call out His namesake Jesus to save those from themselves, for they know not what they are a doing! Blessed is the man that walketh not in the counsel of the ungodly!"

"Okay ... okay, I give up—where do I sign up for the program?" Larry cried uncle.

Not allowing their new friends to go it alone, Tiny and Dave helped the musicians unload the equipment truck. After the task, Tiny handed the boys keys to the band house and invited them back in the morning for breakfast. "We serve from six to ten and make sure you're here. I have something I want to show you heathens and it will make believers out of the both you. And one more thing ..." Tiny pulled a small Bible from his bibs. "I want you to find a Bible verse and read it before you come to breakfast in the morning. These verses written by Paul to the Corinthians will explain a lot about why we do what we do. It is 1st Corinthians 9, verses 19 to 23." Tiny took an index card from his pocket, wrote on it chapter and verse, put the card inside, and handed the Bible to Larry. "It's your first Bible study from your new friend, disciple Tiny," the big guy said with a grin.

Red-eyed and road-weary, Larry and Ed dragged themselves off to the band house for showers and much needed sack time. Before they hit the rack, Larry did what Tiny asked of them, and he read out loud to Ed chapter and verse of 1 Corinthians 9:19–23:

For though I be free from all men, yet have I made myself servant unto all, that I might gain the more. And unto the Jews I became as a Jew, that I might gain the Jews; to them that are under the law, as under the law, that I might gain them that are under the law; To them that are without law, as without law, (being not without law to God, but under the law to Christ,) that I might gain them that are without law. To the weak became I as weak, that I might gain the weak: I am made all things to all men, that I might by all means save some. And this I do for the gospel's sake, that I might be a partaker thereof with you.

Breakfast at Tiny's

Matthew 25:35, 36, 40 (NKJV)

For I was hungry and you gave Me food:

I was thirsty, and you gave Me drink;

I was a stranger and you took Me in;

I was naked, and you clothed Me;

I was sick, And you visited Me;

I was in prison, and you came unto me …

And the King will answer and say to them,

'Assuredly, I say to you, inasmuch as you did it
To one of the least of these My brethren,
you did it to Me.

Too soon the alarm clock broke dream time. Ed, the first to be rousted, caromed a sneaker off Larry's shoulder, smacking the wall beside his head. "What's up with that?" Larry asked, complaining.

"Daylight's burning—it's already nine, dude," Ed griped, and followed pouring out more grievances. "When there's free breakfast we should not be tardy. You realize we haven't had a decent meal since we left 'the burg' … that was eggs and toast two days ago … forty-eight hours without sustenance … we're junk food junkies … vitamin C does not stand for candy or caffeine … sugar rushes are fine for staying awake, but my stomach thinks my throat's been cut. I've got the shakes from eating too much garbage without quality rest."

"I'm up, I am!" Larry cried. "Like an old mother hen you're just cackling away! Brraaack, brraack, brraack!"

Another sneaker barely missed Larry and hit the wall. "Thanks for my other sneaker, Ed. I was wondering where I put that. Good thing your aim isn't spot on ... not unlike your singing ... oooohh!"

Larry had barely tied the sneaker, and not a second too soon, as Ed leaped for Larry's throat but missed and landed on the bed. Larry was the first out the door and down the steps sprinting for the club.

Bursting through the door, Ed was right on Larry's heels. Tiny was serving a table; Dave was behind the grill. The boys blew past, heading for the equipment. "Would you boys like breakfast?" Tiny called out. "Or not?" As the vapor trail of the two lads dissipated, the morning customers went back to their breakfast. Tiny looked at Dave and Dave shrugged his shoulders, "These musicians are a weird lot ... even when it's free they don't seem to care about eating—just their darn music is all. They'll waste away to nuthin'."

Sally, one of the customers who had spiked, and rainbow-colored hair, agreed with Dave, "I used to date one of those so-called musician types. He had some really bizarre habits. A musician for me? HA! HAD 'EM ONCE, AND ... NE-VER A-GAIN!"

Tiny looked at Sally, smiled, and said, "Never thought you the musician type ... a biker maybe?"

"Yeah, maybe next time round ... a biker ... yeah, I like leather. Good idea, Pastor Tiny ... thanks," Sally said with a wink and a smile.

The two boys finally reappeared laughing from out of the darkness from the back of the club.

"Hungry are ya?" Dave asked.

There were pancakes, eggs, sausage, bacon, toast, home fries, gravy, and biscuits, even a few steaks, fresh fruits, and vegetables ... and now two bug-eyed, skinny-as-a-rail musicians gazed longingly down at the vast array of morning vittles displayed before them.

A booming voice suddenly awoke the boys from their foodie dream. "Aaahh, ground control to the Major Toms ... don't drool on the food—sit down. I'll get your drink order, then belly up to the smorgasbord."

After finding two seats among the interesting array of patrons, Tiny asked, "Did you at least read the Bible before coming over this morning?"

"Last night as a bedtime story Larry read me chapter and verse," Ed replied.

"Good deal ... now whudya have fellas?" Tiny asked, and rattled off the menu—coffee, tea, milk, apple juice, grape, orange, cranberry, and good old water. "And, by the way, our head-chef, Dave, will gladly make you a custom omelet, filled and prepared just the way you'd like it."

Dave gave a "Howdy," combined with a spatula salute.

Drinks and eats were on and Ed and Larry pushed food into every nook and cranny that the road trip had shook, rattled, and rolled out of place. They sat back satisfied, and began to assess the environment and who were gathered there. It was a cross between circus and comic strip characters Larry thought. Looking through the window he observed it wasn't motor transport that brought them here, but shopping carts, pull-behind wagons, and bag dollies attached to bi-pedal muscle.

"It's all they got," Tiny said, breaking Larry's wonderment. The big guy sat down and explained. "I take what I gave you to ponder chapter and verse very seriously and it is my mission as I see it. These people are street people. Most of them bed down under overpasses, inside cardboard boxes, or a doorway. If they're really lucky, they make it to the shelter before quota's filled. Sally over there. She made it out, has her own place now and a part time ... cleaned up her drug habit and is now making an honest effort. When she first entered our world, she stumbled in this door and fell flat on her face. Poor girl had been beaten by a trick and shot some contaminated product. Sally would be D. O. A. if she hadn't made it here when she did. She's not a hundred percent yet but she has changed her story. I think her cured but not yet healed."

Ed asked, "Man why do you do this? Some of the smell coming from these folks tells me they haven't the best hygiene. You catch their drift?"

"Just like Christ teaches ... He accepts us just as we are. How can we do anything less? When we approached the owner of this club," Tiny explained, "Asked him if we could do a breakfast ministry three times

114

a week for the homeless, he gave us a dubious eye. But then said, 'Why not?' Of course we had to come up with the food, fixin's, and donations to make it all work. That's week after week, too. But ... when you place it all into the Lord's hands the miracles happen. If you pray for others in His name and be it His will, He blesses manna from heaven abundantly."

"You call this a blessing?" Ed questioned.

"Man, I know it's hard to accept that all this work is a blessing. But if one soul is saved, if one soul is less burdened, it is worth it?" Tiny answered. "I was preaching on the streets, going door-to-door, and one day I stumbled into what I call 'cardboard city.' The big idea light came on and I knew what I had to do. Yeah, the dead-end smell was there, but it smelled sweet and I embraced these forlorn and lost creatures. Thanking Jesus for taking me there, I remembered what is considered great in the eyes of the world is pure folly and foolish to the Creator God. If one does not recognize and help the lowliest of His flock then He will say, 'I knew you not.'"

"Another testimony," Larry said. "You've got a lot of 'em."

"A coin tossed turns many times before it lands. We all have our roads to travel, and our stories to tell," Tiny surmised. "You fellas have yours. Just like Sal you make choices, bend it, shape it ... but your life is not your own

... never was—it is a gift and our gift is to one another ... pursuit of anything else is fool's gold." Tiny paused and added, "Now that we fed the body, we need to feed the spirit! Hey, I've got a morning sermon to preach. Stick around ... it comes with the meal ... like the meal, it's free!"

When Tiny stood up the thirty or so patrons got quiet. They apparently knew what was coming. You could see that the big guy was respected. But he would have told you that it was not the man they respected but the Word that carried him.

First there was a prayer and Tiny asked humbly, claiming that the presence of the Holy Spirit was needed. Thanks were given for the gift of food. Blessings for the people that found their way, and blessings for those searching for sanctuary, forgiveness for all sins past and present were petitioned for.

Then Tiny started the sermon. "Dear friends of 'Choice Ministry,' I want to welcome our regular folks and any new people who have chosen to be a part of our breakfast ministry. I want to introduce to you two rockin'-rollers who made a choice to dine with us this morning. Ed and Larry are here ... stand up fellas."

Ed and Larry stood up and all breakfast diners rubber-necked to check out the mystery guests. There were applause and welcomes given to the wanna- be rock stars. Ed and Larry smiled, waved, and sat down. Larry said to Ed, "I hope that tonight's crowd is as responsive as these poor folks."

"The theme here is ... not how you look, but rather that you showed up and what's in your heart," Ed whispered to Larry.

"I know about darkness," Pastor Tiny started to say, "I have felt despair! I have encountered the specter of loneliness!"

He paused and began again, "There is no passage so narrow, so despondent that we may travel than that of silence and mystery ... that, bearing hours of isolation ... pressed by sorrow ... a place where there is no voice ... no vision ... no sympathy or care ... no hope ... no explanation ... lying face down in a bed of despair ... where the soul cries out ... WHY?"

There were sobs heard coming from the breakfast patrons. Heart strings had been plucked and its music played for all to hear. "YES, WHY?" a shout came from one. "I had everything ... I've lost it all ... my home, my wife, and children. I have been abandoned to walk these streets of pain."

A middle-aged man yelled out, "Yeah, I gotta ask why? Why would such a loving God ... the One you talk about ... wanna hurt us ... the very ones He calls His children ...? Tell me?"

Disciple Tiny stated, "Before I answer that question, let me first say that God does not place upon us any yoke that we cannot bear. For God so loved the world that He gave His only begotten son Jesus Christ to take our place for the sins of the world. Every evil word, thought, and deed from all who have existed upon planet earth ... that includes you and me brother ... He nailed them to the cross ... BANG, debt paid in full. Our debt by His blood He paid for us. As the hammer came down, striking those nine-inch nails ... with every blow, Christ's blood sprayed out covering the earth, metal met metal, His body writhed ... the tree was raised and seated—hours of separation from God the Father continued—faith and hope hanging in the balance. There were no angels or doves hovering about ... absolutely no blessed assurance ... I imagine Satan whispering and taunting ... If you indeed be the Christ, then come down from there ... and the devil recounting every sin of the world to Christ until He cried out ... 'My God, my God, why have You forsaken Me?' Christ did this voluntarily ... the choice of dying, so we may live free, eternally."

Sally, the rainbow, immediately jumped up, raised her hands heavenward, and began to testify, "My brother I know about some things. I know right now you can't see anything but your own pain. I was a prostitute. I had a heroin habit. I hooked because I needed to fix. I was dead when I fell in the door of this place. At first ... it didn't make sense what Pastor Tiny was talking about. What did I have to give to anybody? I'm a whore ... a drug addict. But I made a choice ... either continue what I was doing and die, not knowing true salvation, or inject myself with the water of the living God and crave no more for the things of this world. That's what I did—I leaped into faith, was saved by His grace, and in His promise I do believe. Amen!"

"Amens" resounded from around the room.

The middle-aged man looked at Sally as she sat down, and turned to Pastor Tiny, "Is it that easy, Pastor?"

Sally abruptly spoke up, "I never said it was easy, brother. You have to do your part ... make a choice. You have to be willing. Maybe you haven't hit bottom yet ... can't bounce back 'til ya hit bottom!"

I never said it was easy, brother. You have to do your part ... make a choice. You have to be willing.

"Oh, I've hit bottom, sister," the man stated, assuring the room. "Slept in a box last night, I did ... covered myself up with newspaper and a dank tarp ... woke up with some unwelcome guests ... two rats and a stray dog shared my habitat."

An elderly man laughed and said, "Heh, heh ... when winter comes you'll be glad for three dogs. They keep ya warm and cozy. And they're not as fussy as some women I know about the quality of the box and the company they keep."

All those attending burst into laughter. The elderly man got a sheepish look and then he, too, started to laugh and as he did he revealed that he had no teeth. "Wow," Larry whispered to Ed, "What a crew we've got here."

"Salt of the earth," Ed whispered back. "The salt of the earth. And we are included."

Pastor Tiny calmed everyone down. "All good questions ... all good concerns, and thank you, too, Sally for that great testimony. Friends thank you for being here today and sharing with us. Don't anyone leave here with a heavy heart. Brother Dave and I will be glad to speak to any of you and open the Good Book. We're here to help find answers to those concerns you have. Don't be shy because we're all in the boat of life together."

After Pastor Tiny gave a closing prayer, most of the ragtag group meandered back onto the street. The middle-aged man who sounded out during the sermon hung around. Sally walked over to the man, sat down, and held his hands in hers.

"Need to talk to somebody," the man confided nervously to Sally while looking around the room. "Can't go out there again ... I'm afraid to die. I've been wandering for two weeks now ... shaving's a luxury and I wash myself in gas station bath rooms. Someone stole my only backpack of clothes last night and a bum snuck into my box the other night, getting too familiar with me while I was sleeping." The man broke down sobbing.

Shaking her head that she understood, Sally gently said, "I know all about what you're going through, sir."

"My name's Charlie," the man said between tear drops.

"Okay Charlie ... we'll talk to Pastor Tiny. He'll know just what to do," Sally said, speaking softly trying to calm him down.

Tiny called after Larry and Ed, "I will talk to you guys in a little while!" Exiting the cafe area, they headed to their work, leaving Pastor Tiny and

Dave to theirs. "Man, that's heavy stuff going on. It's a dose of reality that I never want to swallow," Ed mumbled at Larry as they stepped into the cavernous stage area.

"Amen to that fact, Ed. Scary is all I gotta say," agreed Larry. "Here but by the grace of God go we."

CHAPTER 10

Broad and Deep Is the Lord's Kingdom

Establishment of our Lord's reign of grace without real-estate in which it is exercised is a process of futility. The kingdom of God is also the realm in which God's reign may be experienced. Within God's people His rule and reign are made manifest. In our present age we are under attack from the systematic advance of the evil power. The establishment of the kingdom of God here and now can overcome the burgeoning of this cancer.

The kingdom of God can be stated as a doctrine of salvation. It is God exercising His power to defeat evil, thus re-establishing His sovereignty and restore human society to its rightful place of willing subservience to the will of God.

But the kingdom of God is here and now. There is a realm of spiritual blessing that we may enter into today and enjoy by our faith in Jesus Christ. Within our faith lies the realization of hope that today in earth's history the reign of God will not only be received through believers, but will be poured out across the world overcoming satanic powers and establishing God's righteousness.

Only by and through God's grace can we as Christians establish ourselves as citizens of His kingdom. Let's look at two terms used to identify the kingdom of God. 1) The Kingdom of Grace is the present. 2) The Kingdom of Glory is the future.

We will use the term "The Kingdom of Grace" in this chapter. It is the time period after man's fall where it was established and then ratified at Christ's death on the cross, and still today divine grace works on the hearts of mankind. This plan was instituted and devised as a plan of redemption for the guilty race. It existed in purpose by the promise of God. Through faith man becomes the kingdom's subjects. This happens when the hearts of man accept Christ's gift and yield to the sovereignty of God's love.

Grace is a gift, played out in the very midst of us through our knowledge of Jesus and His love. Through your faith, by your belief, you can be made whole as a subject of the kingdom of grace. When you receive the Spirit of God it is the beginning of life eternal. It starts by receiving the prescience of Christ and begins as you enter into rest with Christ Jesus. Matthew 11:28– 30 promises, "Come unto me, all ye that labor and are heavy laden, and I will give you rest. Take my yoke upon you and learn of me; for I am meek and lowly in heart: and ye shall find rest unto your souls. For my yoke is easy, and my burden is light."

Christ seeks to teach us as His disciples the truth that in God's kingdom there are no boundaries or territorial lines, no caste, no aristocracy. This message must be delivered to all nations, kindred, tongues, and people bearing to them the words of a Savior's love.

Principles of development in Christ-like nature are the opposite of those that rule the kingdom of this world. Earthly governments prevail by physical force. But Christ implants a principle of truth and righteousness. He counterworks error and sin.

The plan of salvation was in place long before the creation of earth to redeem man and rescue the world, and when Christ came it was put into operation. This plan was not an afterthought and is played out in Genesis 3:13–15. The covenant of grace was made with man in Eden, when after the fall there was given a divine promise that the seed of the woman (God's church) would bruise the head of the serpent (Satan). To all men this plan offered the hope of salvation.

Man cannot stand on his own. Man cannot achieve salvation by himself. It is only by and through the power of Christ and His infinite mercy for humanity can the difference be made up. Christ's grace is the "get out of jail sin free card" that we all need to hold dear in our hearts.

Christ came to earth, not to change any of God's laws, but to uphold His divine commandments. For God does not change, nor waiver; He is constant and is not confusion or chaos. God is the Alpha and the Omega and everything in between.

It was not merely to accomplish our redemption that Christ came to earth to suffer and die in our stead. He came to magnify the law and make it honorable. It was not just for the worldly inhabitants, but for the whole universe, to see God's law is unchangeable. The death of Christ proves it immutable. The love of the Father and the Son through a sacrifice so great that sinners may be redeemed demonstrates to all beings what nothing less than this plan of atonement could have sufficed to do—that justice and mercy are the very foundation of the law and government of God.

So you pray, "I want to be a Christian in my heart—yes, in my heart … Lord I want to be more loving in my heart … Lord I want to be more holy in my heart … Lord I want to be like Jesus in my heart—in my heart." So you pray this and you sing that and what does it mean to you? Are they wishful, hopeful thoughts prayed and sung only on God's Holy Day? Or have you made them action words of love for Christ Jesus?

Do you have righteousness and peace in the Holy Ghost? Are you a member of Christ's kingdom of grace, a son or daughter of God, a partner in His great firm? Because if you do, my friend, you are a chosen person, elect of God, and a chosen generation. You are peculiar to God Himself, and you are to show forth the praises of Him who is sending you. Because He has called you out of darkness into His marvelous light. By accepting Jesus' grace you are the salt of the earth, a living stone, part of a royal priesthood, and a co-partner with Jesus Christ. Amen.

What is the mission of grace? Is it some sort of mystery? Far from it! It is comprehended by the human mind when enlightened by the Spirit of God. Honesty and a humble heart and the desire to know truth follows acceptance of the gift of salvation. This provides an asylum from the domination of worldly pressure. As such we must live within the system of things, but not be partakers of its evil dimension.

There is a basis for the philosophy of mission for all who become citizens of the kingdom of grace. As you now could think of yourself, through the use of your talents, as a foot soldier fighting for the salvation of the lost and downhearted. Look around you—there are missions everywhere for the benefit of humanity. The same light of grace that has been afforded you is not to be hidden somewhere under a basket. You now have the power and the love of Jesus coursing through your life. Make a difference! Open doors of love for others by giving your testimony about what Jesus' grace has done for you, because you could be the difference in saving many a lost soul.

The greatest teacher to ever set foot on planet earth, Jesus Christ taught by healing, He loved us and understood our human condition. He was God made flesh to walk the same paths we do, speak our language, to be tempted as we are, but He overcame it all to show that it was possible to live without succumbing to evil. He lived by example and knew that not everyone would accept His words.

When you speak to others about Christ's gift and tell your testimony, do not be afraid—not all will accept your new-found faith.

Jesus spoke to the people of that time in parables, in a language that all He was ministering to could understand—He used simple, down-to-earth stories to illustrate divine truths. He spoke about earthly things which the people of the day were most familiar with. Natural things were the medium for the spiritual understanding. His parables are links in the chain of truth that unites man with God and earth with heaven. The kingdom of grace is a work in progress and comes in a form that is a surprise to most. Only those who truly believe will grasp the concept, gladly receive it, and enjoy the peace it brings, and to others it might just be a simple story. Parables bring to light present truth even for our time.

Jesus as a sower went forth to sow the word of God, to plant the seeds of divine love and understanding into the hearts of man. This heavenly grain of truth sown would burst forth as the gospel seed and would bring back man to his loyalty to God.

Matthew 3:3–9:

> And he spake many things unto them in parables, saying, Behold, a sower went forth to sow [This could be you who are reading this book]; And when he sowed, some seeds fell by the way side, and the fowls came and devoured them up: Some fell upon stony places, where they had not much earth: and forthwith they sprung up, because they had no deepness of earth: And when the sun was up, they were scorched; and because they had no root, they withered away. And some fell among the thorns; and the thorns sprung up and choked them: But other fell into good ground, and brought forth fruit, some an hundredfold, some sixtyfold, some thirtyfold. Who hath ears to hear, let him hear.

Matthew 13:37–40: "He that soweth the good seed is the Son of man. The field is the world; the good seed are the children of the kingdom; but the tares are the children of the wicked one. The enemy that sowed them is the devil; the harvest is the end of the world; and the reapers are the angels. As therefore the tares are gathered and burned in the fire; so shall it be in the end of this world."

Christ had come, not as king, but as a sower; not for the overthrow of kingdoms, but for the scattering of seed; not to point His followers to earthly triumphs and national greatness, but to a harvest to be gathered after patient toil, and through losses and disappointments.

Many will listen and understand that the lesson of Christ's parables is a tough one and often unwelcome. It will sound as pounding brass and be a mystery, even though their hearts will be strangely moved, yet the words will so bitterly disappoint their ambitions.

There is hope of understanding, however. And this hope is what Christ desires of all of us. Those who are willing to study the Word of God with open hearts, to the enlightenment of the Holy Spirit, will not remain in darkness as to the meaning of His words. John 7:17 says,

"If any man will do his will, he shall know of the doctrine [teaching], whether it be of God, or whether I speak of myself [Jesus]."

All who come to Christ for a clearer knowledge of truth will receive it. He will reveal the mysteries of the kingdom of grace. These mysteries will be understood by the heart that longs to know the truth. A heavenly light will be given you and shine into your very soul. This heavenly light will be revealed to those around you as a bright, shining lamp on a dark path. Amen.

As you go through this life trying to sow the seeds of God's love, hope, and encouragement, remember that, much to your surprise, there will be those around you who really will accept Christ's message. Unfortunately, the percentages of disappoints will be many. As Christ explained the parable of the sower in Mark 4:13–24 to His disciples, He asked them, If you do not understand this story, how then will you know any parable? Therefore, He gave the explanation:

The sower soweth the word [the Gospel of Jesus Christ]. And these are they by the way side, where the word is sown; but when they have heard, Satan cometh immediately, and taketh away the word that was sown in their hearts. And these are they likewise which are sown on stony ground; who, when they have heard the word, immediately receive it with gladness; And have no root in themselves, and so endure but for a time: afterward, when affliction or persecution ariseth for the word's sake, immediately they are offended. And these are they which are sown among thorns; such as hear the word, And the cares of this world, and the deceitfulness of riches, and the lusts of other things entering in, choke the word, and it becometh unfruitful. And these are they which are sown on good ground; such as hear the word, and receive it, and bring forth fruit, some thirtyfold, some sixty, and some an hundred. And He said unto them, Is a candle brought to be put under a bushel, or under a bed? and not be set on a candlestick? For there is nothing hid, which shall not be manifested; neither was any thing kept secret, but that it should come abroad. If any man have ears to hear, let him hear. And He said unto them, Take heed what ye hear: with what measure ye mete [judge fairly in all matters], it shall be measured to you: and unto you that hear shall more be given.

Remember, as you spread the Word of God there will be many who disagree, many who will condemn, many who will turn their backs and slam doors in your face. However, God has not committed to us the work of judging character or motive; in other words, it is not our job to figure out who the tares are—or who is not. That is not your cross to bear. These parables are given for humility and distrust of self, for forbearance and tender, loving care for all, not for judgement and condemnation of others due to their shortcomings. This is the walk of Jesus Christ for all those who desire to live within the kingdom of grace.

Faith as in the parable of the mustard seed is what is needed. A mustard seed? That is so tiny, almost insignificant ... but see how it grows. And that is the point. "Another parable put he [Jesus] forth unto them, saying, The kingdom of heaven is like to a grain of mustard seed, which a man [Son of God] took, and sowed in his field [the world]: Which indeed is the least of all seeds: but when it is grown, it is the greatest among herbs, and becometh a tree, so that the birds of the air come and lodge in the branches thereof" (Matt. 13:31, 32).

The principles of God's kingdom of grace are peculiar to the development of His kingdom. Therein it is not by those who rule the kingdoms of the world, prevailing through brute force and maintain their dominions by threat of war. God does not compel conscience by force.

Christ's kingdom of grace in its inception seemed humble, insignificant, the least of all things—as the mustard seed. And compared to earthly dominions it was hardly noticed. The work of grace in the heart is small in the beginning. It starts from within and moves outward. The works of truth continue when planted, in secret, silent and steady, pervading all the faculties of the soul, and nourishing all the kingdoms of the world with God's divine truth.

"Marvelous Grace" ... the last verse of this song compels one to pause:

Marvelous, infinite, matchless grace,

Freely bestowed to all who believe!

You that are longing to see His face,

Will you this moment His grace receive?

Grace, grace, God's grace,

Grace that will pardon and cleanse within;

Grace, grace, God's grace,

Grace that is greater than all our sin!

(Julia Johnson, 1911)

Accepting Christ's free gift of grace is the first step. You cannot restore the image of God within yourself by yourself. It must be in harmony with God's principles working from within outward before you can be fitted for the kingdom of glory. The heart needs to be right, converted, and sanctified. True obedience springs forth from the love of righteousness—love of the law of God.

You cannot restore the image of God within yourself by yourself. It must be in harmony with God's principles working from within outward before you can be fitted for the kingdom of glory.

The essence of all righteousness is loyalty to our Redeemer, Jesus Christ. He simply leads us to do right because it is right ... because doing right is pleasing to God, and we do what is right because we love Jesus. Before I knew and loved Jesus, He died—gave up His life so that I may have life eternal. I, too, was washed clean and made whole through the blood of His sacrifice as He did for all mankind.

127

A Story Within ... The Story of Rueben Versus

Meyer

The first day of my new life was a day of immense blessing. I stopped looking at my past as a total life of regret. I felt as I had overcome. You who are reading this must realize that this author did not just suddenly give up and overcome his worldly addictions. No, I confess that I am a "WIP"— Work in Progress.

Do you have a bad habit or addiction? Are you thinking, "Oh, God doesn't care about lil' ol' me?" Stop thinking that and stop blaming yourself for all your past shortcomings—because you have been forgiven. The hardest thing to do is to forgive yourself, even though God has already done that and more. Toss it out like yesterday's trash and move on. You can do it with God's help.

Is it about doing too much ... gotta do this, go there, overkill kind of addiction. Or is it the opposite, lethargic kind of addiction ... woe is me ... coulda', shoulda, but just can't git 'er dun? Everything is possible to overcome, little by little, day by day ... a long journey always starts with the first step. I know ... cliché, cliché, but it applies. Start the day asking the Lord to hold you up, to give you the courage to move off point and... read the Bible. Most times after prayer, BINGO ... right there in the Scriptures you will find the answer. I know as it has happened to me, just when I needed it most.

Try becoming more forgiving; repair those hurting relationships. Talk to people with genuine kindness and sincerity. No one else will care until they honestly know how much you care.

Want to kick that old habit? Replace it by starting a new, good habit. There's no better time than right now to make a vow, make a true commitment to stop hurting yourself. God is the one constant who never changes—He will walk beside you every step of the way through life, and if at times you look down and see only one set of footprints on the path and wonder, "Where did He go? where is He?" Remember that those were the times that He was carrying you.

FORSAKE: Transitive verb. Forgo: leave or abandon.

Nehemiah 9:17: "But you are a forgiving God, gracious and compassionate, slow to anger and abounding love. Therefore you did not desert [forsake] them" (NIV).

DESPAIR: Noun. loss of hope, lose all hope—despairing (adjective).

Psalm 42:11: "Why art thou cast down, O my soul? and why art thou disquieted within me? hope thou in God; for I shall yet praise Him, who is the health of my countenance, and my God."

DESOLATE: Adjective. forsaken; dismal, dreary; forlorn— Lay waste; devastate (transitive verb)—desolation (noun).

Proverbs 3:25, 26: "Be not afraid of sudden fear, neither of the desolation of the wicked, when it cometh. For the Lord shall be thy confidence, and keep thy foot from being taken."

This is a true story based on true events which were related to me by Mr. Meyer in the 1980s. The whodunnit name has been changed and some creative license has been exercised throughout the story line. However, the facts are true and the outcome a blessed example of how we should treat our brothers and sisters. Amen.

The Story ...

Cold sweat outlined Rueben's furrowed brow as he blankly stared through the rain-spattered window glass of the police cruiser. Hot air blasted from the car's heating system but did little to fend off the nerved chill from his body.

Wringing his handcuffed hands, Rueben squirmed trying to find a more comfortable seating position. The cutting edges of the metal restraints sent a bleak message of stark reality.

"Was this a joke?" Rueben asked himself. "No joke," he answered internally. "What brought me here?" Rueben pondered.

Wasn't there a warning for poor old Rueben before the worm hole spit him onto this bridge of sighs? This was no house party or traffic citation; this event surely should never have been included on Rueben's bucket list of things to do.

A cannon shot burst like last summer's fireworks and echoed the day's events in Rueben's mind. Might there be a "get out of jail free card" stashed away somewhere in this fateful deck of cards to be played? Rueben agitated by all his negative answers, shuffled his feet, shook his head, peered at the floor, and mumbled, "Not today ... no, not today."

DESPAIR ...

"What's that you say?" asked the trooper in the front seat.

Wrestling with the uncomfortable feeling of imminent doom Rueben replied, "I was just saying that it's been a long day."

"It'll be an even longer night by the time you get booked and tucked away," the trooper flatly stated.

"My head is pounding ... I took a pretty good hit. You guys got any aspirin or anything?" Rueben lamented.

"You could ask the store owner you met earlier tonight. I am sure he's feeling gracious right about now. After all it was just a small can of beans that knocked you flat instead of a bullet from a forty-four," the officer smirked.

The flippant remark only worsened the heartbeat throb of pain from the goose-egg size bump on the back of his head. Looking through the window glass, Rueben squinted to see the other officer questioning the store owner. He mentally mulled over the past several hours' events.

It was a simple idea, really. Rueben had planned this all out earlier in the day. This store was a little off the beaten path. He didn't want to hurt anyone ... just walk in at closing time, hopefully nobody around except the cashier, pretend he had a gun, and say, "Hand over the cash!" He'd be quickly out the door.

But nnnoooo, that wasn't how it all went down. The old boy garnered a little more pluck than Rueben was ready to handle. And how did he suspect that was only a pointy finger in the fabric of his jacket pocket instead of a gun? Yes, how'd he known that? The hurt was so ridiculous it almost made poor Rueben cry.

Continuing on the rewind ... yes, he did it. He walked right into that little country store and started doing the robbery thing. Rueben warned the old fellow not to come out from behind the counter, but he did it anyway. He didn't consider the "rollie-pollie" man as any threat, but Rueben discovered he had a lot more muscle when they began to tussle. End caps were knocked over. Groceries went flying off shelves. Finally Rueben managed to get unlocked from the old guy and headed for the door and that's when the lights went out. He didn't know at the time of unconsciousness, but when he woke up he found that he had been struck out by a fastball—a well-thrown, 18.5 oz. can of baked beans ... *and you're out!*

A loud, complaining grumble emanated from the officer in the front seat, "Alright ... hold on fella, lemme' see what I can get out of the store for your headache. Stay put and don't do anything stupid. I don't want to chase after ya a second time and especially not in this weather!"

Psalm 9:9: "The Lord also will be a refuge for the oppressed, a refuge in times of trouble."

Could any good ever come from this horrible situation? Rueben wondered. Oooohhh ... Mr. Big-Time Rueben brought down by a well- aimed can of baked beans. The boys on the block are gonna love this new jailhouse story. "Whud'ya in for, kid?" they'll question, and "How'd they nab ya?" they'll ask. But they will all know before I arrive. So I gotta tell it true. Probably they'll scoff and say, "Hey, here comes Mr. Bean ... the new beanie-weenie, the lean, mean, bean man ... boy did he get beaned! Ha! Ha! Ha!"

It was just less than fifteen hours ago that Rueben was enjoying his daily routine; a stale cup of the prior evenings "Joe" sat before him as he inhaled his first cigarette of the day. Nothing new on the early report; same old junk ... people out of work, more homeless than shelters can hold, bad weather and earthquakes, people around the planet are at war with each other. Yeah, everything was pretty much normal.

"You going out today?" was Rueben's wife's question, startling him from his routine. "Maybe you are thinking of going out today ... to find work?" The inquisition continued, "Maybe hit the unemployment office ... or signing up for some assistance? I would do it myself, but I already have gainful employment. The least you could do is to help us get out of financial misery rather than add to the problem, Rueben. It is all I can do to keep food on the table … are you even listening to a word I've said? Unglue yourself from that stupid TV … better yet, turn it off!"

"Wow, sweetheart … you know I love you, too, honey," Rueben replied and added, "It is really nice to see you alive and looking so fine this morning!"

"Shut up Rueb … stop playing me the fool and yourself … just try and help out somehow … surprise me today and do the right thing, okay?" his wife said and called to him over her shoulder as she hurried off to work. "The right thing."

Rueben blinked when the door closed with some authority. The early morning vitriol had interrupted his deep thoughts. He winced as he took another sip of coffee and exclaimed to an empty house, "Don't I always … sweetheart, do the right thing?" Exhaling the cigarette's last breath, he stubbed it out in the overflowing ashtray and stood up. In his mind he remembered casing a nearby grocery; he beheld a plan and a smile crossed his lips. Rueben was ready to go the distance … yup, the right thing to do.

The sound of the opening car door reeled Rueben in from his daydream and the officer barked an order. "Look here, I've got some aspirin and the store-keep was nice enough to give some water … open up and I'll feed 'em to ya, and no monkey business. Hear me?"

After washing down the pills with a few gulps of water Rueben thanked the officer.

The officer hesitated and stated, "There is one more thing, too," the trooper tersely added, "And it is off the charts as far as I am concerned, but the store owner insisted and wants to say something to ya. Don't give him no guff, understand? The fella seems sincere and kind enough and that's why I'm lettin' it happen." After that being said the officer moved out of the way. And there stood the store owner. Yup, for sure it was the "rollie- pollie" guy who just a few hours earlier Rueben in all his glory had tried to rob.

"What a situation," Rueben thought to himself. Did he want to scream at him? Did he want to tell him what a stupid jerk he was? What else could he or would he want to do or say? Rueben mentally tried to prepare for the comin' right at you, in your face, inevitable verbal barrage.

Suddenly the good old boy was leaning towards Rueben ready to speak. But wait a minute ... was this an illusion? Was there a welling of tears in the man's eyes? When he began to speak, he spoke not words of anger ... was it pity? ... no this was forgiveness. "Son," the man started out, "My name's Meyer and I just want to say that if you ever need anything, all you have to do is ask. If you had came into my store this evening and explained your situation to me, I would have helped. If you needed food, I would have filled a cart for you and then some. Whatever was troubling you, together we would have found an answer. Never did it have to end like this. I would like to be placed on your visitation list if you would allow. You don't have to answer now ... just think about it."

"God bless you, son," were Mr. Meyer's parting words as the door to the police cruiser closed.

Who's the big dog now? Rueben pondered. *And who's the tough guy?* The tears Rueben saw in Mr. Meyer's eyes now took up real estate in his.

"And Jesus wept," Rueben mumbled, "And why now do I remember it? Certainly I did not hear it down at Clancy's Bar. And why would Jesus weep for me, anyway?" Rueben continued his monologue, "My wife is soon gonna wonder where I am and when she finds out its end game ... D-I-V-O-R-C-E. Ain't never gonna see my kids again. Now I know where I saw 'Jesus wept' ... it was in one of those coloring books the kids brought home from church."

Rueben cringed as he recalled what his wife said as she was going out the door and headed for church. "Turn off that TV and come along with us. Times all we got and we shouldn't be wasting it. It's too short ... someday sooner than later you are going to regret it. You can never get these precious moments back, Rueb."

He remembered the questioning looks, all too vivid now, that the kids would give him ... every time they wanted to do something together as a family. Perhaps the kids were asking, "Don't you love us enough, Dad, to spend time with us?" Rueben gritted his teeth, "Wow, this is heavy ... why all this stuff now? I guess I've got use of precious time to sort this out now."

Suddenly the front doors to the police cruiser opened and the two officers slid into their respective positions. The officer in the passenger's side turned and asked, "Are you a first timer with no warrants pending?"

"Yeah," Rueben muttered.

"Well, it's not going to be a hard ride," the trooper quipped. "No priors ... no use of a hand-gun ... just a botched attempt at thievery. The store-keep said you two tussled a bit, but he's not even making that an issue."

The driver summed it up rather smugly, "You are one lucky offender," and then asked, "What kind of plan did you have in place ... I mean what were you thinking ... or maybe the fact is you weren't?"

"Guess there really wasn't much of a plan," Rueben admitted and explained, "My family needed food and I haven't had a job in months. Hearing about it all the time from my wife doesn't make me feel much like the man of the house that I should be. She's got a job, and I don't. She provides, and I don't. That's it, but it wasn't always that way. Don't take it wrong ... I know how it sounds—I ain't feeling sorry for myself. I haven't asked anybody for anything that I haven't earned or that's not mine, but for the sake of earning it. Today was the day I guess I went over the edge. I'm sorry it happened and here I am sitting in the back of your fine police car."

"No, Rueben, actually," the trooper in the passenger's side corrected his observation, "It's your police car, too. This vehicle right here is paid for in part by your tax dollars and honestly on your payroll. So I guess you could say that tonight we protected you from yourself. I hope that we have made you feel right at home and treated you as fair as we possibly could."

Rueben smiled and thought, *these two are a real dynamic comedy duo.* He considered that what the trooper said was correct. It was true that the equipment and officers were provided by and for the people. There was some real irony in that, too. He guessed that it was the two officers' job to protect the public and Rueben from the ways of his error.

And so it was the arraignment was attended by Mr. Meyer and Rueben's wife. He had not spoken to her since his one gratuitous phone call. That conversation was brief and to the point and pretty much it was only he who spoke—what had happened ... where he ended up. She was oddly quiet. He asked about the kiddos, but there was silence on her part and then came that thunderous click. Waves of milliseconds roared by as Rueben stood with the phone's receiver pressed tightly to his ear, praying for a different outcome ... listening to the hum of a communication line now gone dead.

FORSAKEN ...

An uneasy, nerved coldness stalked Rueben as he shuddered before the judge. This conversation, too, was brief as the court-appointed attorney stated no contest—guilty as charged. The sentence was delivered ... the gavel came down, but leniency was granted due to the fact of first offense. Rueben was elated and thankful because in his heart he knew that this would be a once and done. This would never happen again. As he turned to share his good fortune his smile faded. His wife had already slipped away. However the "rollie-pollie" shop keeper was still there and gave Rueben a smile. Cuffs were now placed on Rueben, and the court officer moved him along to be transported to county for a few months.

Rueben was elated and thankful because in his heart he knew that this would be a once and done. This would never happen again.

ISOLATION ...

Thirteen long days passed by for Rueben ... visitation times came and went without visitors, without incident. Unhappily camping out at the county prison, Rueben was desperately hoping that at least one of his phone calls would be answered ... but never was that the case. His home phone was never picked up. He had no use for an attorney at this point. So there was no need to speak with anyone in that regard. When he was invited to chapel service he declined. Rueben pretty much kept to himself as much as possible. When it was time to mix with the general population he would stay in his cell and play solitaire or hearts with his elderly cellmate who was in for DUI.

Then one day ... a guard came tapping on his cell door, "Hey Rueben, you got a visitor."

"Is it my wife and kids?" Rueben excitedly asked.

"No, it's some guy ... name of Meyer, I think," answered the guard and added, "He's on your visit list—you want to take it or not? You got twenty."

Putting down his hand of cards, Rueben shuffled towards the door, leaned on the bars, and said somberly, "Yeah, I guess ... why not?"

Going through security was a task in and of itself—buzzers buzzed, locks turned, gates were drawn back, and voices on intercoms verified who, what, where, and how long.

"Rueben, number fifteen," a guard shouted. Moving towards table fifteen, Rueben sat down. Yup, it was the man from the grocery store. In front of Mr. Meyer, laying on the table, was a brown paper bag.

First he looked at Mr. Meyer, then he looked at the paper bag. Mr. Meyer was the first to speak and asked the obvious first-time visitation question: "So, how are things? But maybe that is a stupid question? How are you holding up under the circumstances? Know that these aren't frivolous questions as I am honestly concerned ... I want you to know that, I hope you know that."

Again, Rueben eyed the man and looked down, stared at the package, and answered, "Yeah, I think you are sincere ... not sure why ... but I do. Don't think I don't appreciate the visit ... I do. It's just ... and I think you can tell by my demeanor that ... well, I was kinda hoping to see someone else here long before this and they ain't showed up yet. I suppose they're thinkin' I ain't worth the visit. Or, maybe they plainly, simply wrote me off as a bad investment. But hey, what's in this for you? I mean, what do you get out of coming to see a jail bird?"

"Nothing's in it for me, Rueben, but who are you looking for?" asked Meyer.

"My wife and kids," Rueben replied.

"Oh," said Meyer. "That's hard ... I am sorry. You never know ... she might have a change of heart. Some things take a time of understanding and healing. She might be in shock over this business and needs time to think and sort things out. I can see that you miss them ... I don't even need to ask."

Hesitating, Rueben then said, "More than I would have ever thought ... I have missed out on so much of family life and I don't understand why. But if I ever get a second chance I will hold on tight and cherish every second of that precious time. Because as my wife tried to tell me once ... you can never get those moments back."

Proverbs 16:9: "A man's heart plans his way, but the LORD directs his steps" (NKJV).

DESOLATION ...

Mr. Meyer smiled and said. "Life is a funny thing, Rueben. It turns on a dime. What you think may be an unfortunate turn of events could turn out to be a blessing in disguise ... if you look at it the right way."

"Well, right now Mr. Meyer," said Rueben, "And looking at it from this side of the room, it appears as a pretty grim reality and I am not too happy about the fix I'm in or my future prospects. I let a lotta people down, but mostly myself. They say if I show good behavior and co-operate, I could be outta here in three months. But man, this will be the longest three months of my life. I could get out even earlier than that on work release if I had a job and someone to vouch for me. But, that ain't never gonna happen."

"Would you mind if I pray for you?" asked Mr. Meyer.

"When? Right here ... right now? In front of these other jail rats?" questioned Rueben, looking at Mr. Meyer as if he might be crazy.

"Would you be embarrassed?" asked Mr. Meyer and then added, "Even the biggest and meanest character can be brought down by prayer and a little faith. Ever read the story about David and Goliath? No challenge is too big for the Lord, Rueben. You need just use a little faith and rest your troubles upon the Lord's shoulders for a while and forget about YOU. And hey ... I know that's easier said than done."

Rueben considered the offer for prayer, put it on hold, and looked at the brown paper bag, then asked, "Ah, what's in the bag, Mr. Meyer?"

"It could be the roadmap to a brighter future if you allow it to be," Mr. Meyer said. First looking at the guard who had inspected the parcel before allowing it in, he got the nod and then pushed it to Rueben.

Now opening the bag Rueben removed from it a King James Bible. He noted that his name had been engraved on the cover.

Rueben held the Bible in two hands and was very quiet. Mr. Meyer then broke the silence, "I know you could have probably used a carton of cigarettes right now, but this is the best habit I could propose to help you more in the long haul. Doesn't matter on what page, chapter, or verse you start, just get started. Read here a little, there a little, and soon you won't be able to put it down. You will find there is nothing new under the sun and you haven't done anything worse than those who are written about in this book ... probably less. Love the Lord with all your heart, all your soul, and all your mind ... keep His commandments, treat others as you would want to be treated ... that's it in a nutshell."

Rueben looked at Mr. Meyer and Mr. Meyer at Rueben. There were tears in Rueben's eyes that he tried to cover up as he asked, "Would you pray for me now?"

"Now and every day, until you get out of here and thereafter," stated Mr.

Meyer. "That being the gospel truth that you can bank on, Rueben."

Rueben took Mr. Meyer's advice and diligently dove into the reading of the Bible. He prayed and read and prayed some more and began the long walk to cleansing his heart. In a few weeks work release was arranged by a man he didn't even know. Two months later another of Rueben's prayers was answered. His wife surprised him with a visitation.

Rueben, through tears of joy, asked, "What changed your mind about coming to see me?"

"I woke up in the middle of the night and thought about you sitting in here all alone and I felt a change of heart. But before I bring the children," she asserted, "I wanted to see you face-to-face. But know this, Rueben, I do miss you, too. And somehow I hear a change in your heart and I see a change in your eyes. They reflect some new-found sincerity and, since you asked, yes, I forgive you."

True to the words he spoke to his wife in the visitation room, Rueben remained diligent in daily devotional study and prayer, for not only himself, but his family as well. One day soon after his release from jail, he gathered his wife and two children and took them on a short trip to a little out-of-the- way country store. Upon entering the store there was Mr. Meyer in the same exact spot where he and Rueben had first met so many months before.

This time was different. Rueben was not there out of desperation, and puzzled to say the least was his wife—she couldn't understand the reason why they had come so far out of the way to buy groceries. He had never told her until now about the important role Mr. Meyer played in his survival behind bars.

Rueben then said to his family, "I want to introduce you to my new brother, Mr. Meyer, who turned my life around and introduced me to our Lord and Savior Jesus Christ."

John 14:13–14 says, "And whatsoever ye shall ask in my name, that will I do, that the Father may be glorified in the Son. If ye shall ask any thing in my name, I will do it."

Every day we have new opportunities to make a difference. Every day we are faced with challenges. It is up to us to make right choices for the benefit of one another. Humankind is our business, and how we fit into that process is our choice. Treat one another as you would want to be treated and put God first in all you do and say. Ask, "What would Jesus do?" Amen.

This small story is like many we see in the world today. But it is those who want to make a difference in other's lives, doing so without gain, without expecting return of kind, that reflects Christ's love for humanity.

FAITH: "And Jesus answering saith unto them, Have faith in God. For verily I say unto you, That whosoever say unto this mountain, Be thou removed, and be thou cast into the sea; and shall not doubt it in his heart, but shall believe that those things which he saith shall come to pass; he shall have whatsoever he saith. Therefore I say unto you, what things soever ye desire, when ye pray, believe that ye receive them, and ye shall have them. And when ye stand praying, forgive, if ye have ought against any: that your Father also which is in heaven may forgive you your trespasses. But if ye do not forgive, neither will your Father which is in heaven forgive your trespasses" (Mark 11:22–26).

HOPE: "In thee, O LORD, do I put my trust: let me never be put to confusion. Deliver me in thy righteousness, and cause me to escape: incline thine ear unto me, and save me … For thou art my hope, O Lord God: thou art my trust from my youth. … But I will hope continually, and will yet praise thee more and more. My mouth shall shew forth thy righteousness and thy salvation all the day; for I know not the numbers thereof" (Psalm 71:1–2, 5, 14–15).

CHARITY: "And now abideth faith, hope, charity, these three; but the greatest of these is charity" (1 Corinthians 13:13).

TRUST: "Trust in the Lord, and do good; so shalt thou dwell in the land, and verily thou shalt be fed. Delight thyself also in the LORD: and He shall give thee the desires of thine heart. Commit thy way unto the Lord; trust also in him; and he shall bring it to pass" (Psalm 37:3-5).

"In the beginning was the Word, and the Word was with God, and the Word was God. The same was in the beginning with God. All things were made by him; and without him was not anything made that was made. In him was life; and the life was the light of men. And the light shineth in darkness; and the darkness comprehended it not" (John 1:1–5).

Epilogue

L astly everyone wonders ... when I make the commitment to begin change, taking a new pathway to better my life, where do I go from that point on? How do I fill the void left over from my old ways?

Daily, one step at a time, you will begin anew. With prayer, with study, and soon it becomes routine. Included in these last few thoughts and verses are words of encouragement that will shore up the discoveries and conclusions dealt with in the past story.

Let no man guide you—all things devised by man are prone to eventual failure. Listen to God speak to you through the Holy Scriptures. Let the Holy Spirit guide you ... listen and hear His Word:

So from now on we regard no one from a worldly point of view. Though we once regarded Christ in this way, we do so no longer. Therefore, if anyone is in Christ, the new creation has come: the old has gone, the new is here! All this is from God, who reconciled us to himself through Christ and gave us the ministry of reconciliation: that God was reconciling the world to himself in Christ, not counting people's sins against them. And He has committed to us the message of reconciliation. We are therefore Christ's ambassadors, as though God were making his appeal through us. We implore you on Christ's behalf: Be reconciled to God. God made Him who had no sin to be sin for us, so that in him we might become the righteousness of God. (2 Corinthians 5:16–21, NIV)

2 Corinthians 6:1–2: "As God's co- workers we urge you not to receive God's grace in vain. For he says, 'In the time of my favor I heard you, and in the day of salvation I helped you'" (NIV).

Psalm 37:37: "Consider the blameless, observe the upright; a future awaits those who seek peace" (NIV).

Galatians 5:16: "This I say then, Walk in the Spirit, and ye shall not fulfil the lust of the flesh."

1 John tells us to stop loving the world with all its evil intentions. In Ephesians 1:19 we find a prayer for us to begin to understand the amazing greatness of God's power for those who believe in Him. And finally, Lamentations gives us the blessed hope of God's great faithfulness for His mercy begins anew each and every day.

And how about all of us looking at each other and seeing only people as the covers of many books? Each book holds a story inside, you know. We've all heard the saying, "Don't judge a book by its cover." Each one has a unique beginning and eventually there is the end. It is what we do within each chapter that counts. Have you personally ever fallen down? No? Then how would you know what it takes to brush yourself off, shake off the past mistakes, get back up, and re-boot, jumpstarting the story of your life, fresh and new?

Show me someone who has never made a mistake and I will show you a person who has never lived. There is only one person who has lived a perfect life and in His teaching is where we need to place our trust. Worldly experience comes rife with pitfalls and dilemmas. The everyday decision- making process places us in situations that lead us to believe there is nowhere to hide and no one to turn to—that life has suddenly taken us down a dead-end street. Everyone has felt this—no one is immune. Let it not lead to stifling of life but rather stand strong and today start a new and blessed beginning.

The Blessed Effects of Justification—Romans 5:1– 11:

> Therefore being justified by faith, we have peace with God through our Lord Jesus Christ. By whom we also have access by faith into this grace wherein we stand, and rejoice in hope of

the glory of God. And not only so, but we glory in tribulations also: knowing that tribulation worketh patience; And patience, experience; and experience, hope: And hope maketh not ashamed; because the love of God is shed abroad in our hearts by the Holy Ghost which is given unto us. For when we were yet without strength, in due time Christ died for the ungodly. For scarcely for a righteous man will one die: yet peradventure for a good man some would even dare to die. But God commendeth his love toward us, in that, while we were yet sinners, Christ died for us. Much more then, being now justified by his blood, we shall be saved from wrath through him. For if, when we were enemies, we were reconciled to God by the death of his Son, much more, being reconciled, we shall be saved by his life. And not only so, but we also joy in God through our Lord Jesus Christ, by whom we have now received the atonement.

Justification Means Complete Pardon—Romans 3:24–26:

And all are justified freely by his grace through the redemption that came by Christ Jesus. God presented Christ as a sacrifice of atonement, through the shedding of his blood—to be received by faith. He did this to demonstrate his righteousness, because in his forbearance he had left the sins committed beforehand unpunished—he did it to demonstrate his righteousness at the present time, so as to be just and the one who justifies those who have faith in Jesus. (NIV)

Here the truth is laid out in plain lines. This mercy and goodness is wholly undeserved. The grace of Christ is freely given to justify the sinner without merit or claim on his part. Justification is a full, complete pardon of sin. The moment a sinner accepts Christ by faith, that moment he is pardoned. The righteousness of Christ is imputed to him, and he is to no more doubt God's forgiving grace.

There is nothing in faith that makes it our savior. Faith cannot remove our guilt. Christ is the power of God unto salvation to all them that believe. The justification comes through the merits of Jesus Christ. He has paid the price for the sinner's redemption. Yet it is only through faith in His blood that Jesus can justify the believer.

The sinner cannot depend upon his own good works as a means of justification. He must come to the point where he will renounce all his sin, and embrace one degree of light after another, as it shines upon his pathway. He simply grasps by faith the free and ample provision made in the blood of Christ. He believes the promises of God which through Christ are made unto him sanctification and righteousness and redemption.

And if he follows Jesus, he will walk humbly in the light, rejoicing in the light, and diffusing that light to others. Being justified by faith, he carries cheerfulness with him in his obedience in all his life. Peace with God is the result of what Christ is to him. The souls who are in subordination to God, who honor Him, and are doers of His Word, will receive divine enlightenment. In the precious Word of God, there is purity and loftiness as well as beauty that, unless assisted by God, the highest powers of man cannot attain to. (White, Signs of the Times, May 19, 1898)

Amen.

Bibliography

"Joint Declaration on the Doctrine of Justification," Wikipedia, **http://1ref.us/ri** (accessed 1/21/2019)

Luther, Martin. *Luther's Large Catechism* (1529).

Mosheim, Johann. *Institutes of Ecclesiastical History, Ancient and Modern,* book three (1755).

Strong, Josiah. *Our Country* (1885).

Thomaston, J.L Day. Letter, **http://1ref.us/rj** (accessed 12/23/2018). White, Ellen G. *The Acts of the Apostles.* Mountain View, CA: Pacific

Press Publishing Association, 1911.

White, Ellen G. *Christian Temperance and Bible Hygiene.* Battle Creek, MI: Good Health Publishing Company, 1890.

White, Ellen G. *Counsels on Diet and Foods.* Washington, DC: Review and Herald Publishing Association, 1938.

White, Ellen G. *The Great Controversy.* Mountain View, CA: Pacific Press Publishing Association, 1911.

White, Ellen G. Letter 63 (1898).

White, Ellen G. Manuscript 55 (1900).

White, Ellen G. "Purpose of Man's Creation." *Review and Herald* (Feb. 11, 1902).

White, Ellen G. *The SDA Bible Commentary.* Vol. 5. Washington, DC: Review and Herald Publishing Association, 1956.

White, Ellen G. *Selected Messages,* vol 1. Washington, DC: Review and Herald Publishing Association, 1958.

White, Ellen G. *Spiritual Gifts.* Vol. 4. Battle Creek, MI: Seventh-day Adventist Publishing Association, 1864.

www.ingramcontent.com/pod-product-compliance
Lightning Source LLC
Chambersburg PA
CBHW051203120626
46547CB00012B/1183